20
86
Neuer Garten
HAVEL
Nikolskoer Weg
BERLINER
Königstr.
62
HEILIGER SEE
58
Glienicker Brücke
Königstr.
36
Berliner Str.
50
FORST
10
Behlertstr.
Karl-Marx-Str.
PARK BABELSBERG
Glienicke
nach
92
Allee
Berliner Str.
HAVEL
GRIEBNITZSEE
98
Nuthestr.
Babelsberg-Nord
Karl-Marx-Str.
Alt Nowawes
Rudolf-Breitscheid-Str.
100
Griebnitzsee
abelsberger Str.
Rudolf-
Breitscheid-Str.
Friedrich-List-Str.
Babelsberg
Großbeerenstr.
August-Bebel-Str.
Heinrich-Mann-Allee
Nuthestr.
Teltower Vorstadt
Babelsberg
Großbeerenstr.
44
Heinrich-Mann-Allee
Nuthestr.
Heinrich-Mann-Allee

Clemens Beeck
Günter Schneider (Photos)

Potsdam
Highlights

The Practical Guide for
Discovering the City

Jaron Verlag

We would like to thank the Foundation of Prussian Palaces and Gardens of Berlin-Brandenburg (SPSG) for its kind support.

The photographs of the following sites were taken with the permission of the SPSG: Babelsberg Palace and Park, Picture Gallery, Caputh Palace, Cecilienhof Palace, Charlottenhof Palace, Roman Baths, Steam Engine Building, Church of Peace, Marly Gardens, Glienicke Palace and Park, Stern Hunting Lodge, Marble Palace, New Garden, New Orangery, Belvedere on the Klausberg, New Palace, Paretz Palace, Pfingstberg, Ruinenberg, Historic Mill, Sacrow Palace and Sanssouci Palace and Park.

Illustrations
Front cover: Chinese House (Sanssouci Park)
Page 2: Cupola on St. Nicholas Church and Fortuna Portal (City Palace)
Page 6: Sanssouci Palace with vineyard terraces
Page 109: Roman Bath in Park Sanssouci
Back cover (from left above): Inner courtyard of Roman Baths, Brandenburg Gate, Lettering on the Sanssouci Palace, East wing of Picture Gallery

First edition
1st printing 2018

(Original title: "Highlights in Potsdam. Der praktische Begleiter für Entdeckungstouren durch die Stadt")

www.jaron-verlag.de
Translation: Miriamne Fields, Berlin
Map (Page 1): Matthias Frach, Berlin
Public transportation map (Page 112): ViP Verkehrsbetrieb Potsdam GmbH
Cover design: Bauer+Möhring, Berlin, using photos by Günter Schneider
Typesetting: Prill Partners | producing, Barcelona
Lithography: Bild1Druck GmbH, Berlin
Print and binding: Westermann Druck Zwickau GmbH, Zwickau

ISBN 978-3-89773-847-8
ISBN 978-3-89773-848-5 (5 copies)

Potsdam's Highlights – Between Crown and Culture

The name Potsdam once stood for Prussia, a kingdom that has long ceased to exist. The royal heads continued to shape and design the city in the state of Brandenburg to their own taste until the November Revolution in 1918, when the Hohenzollern dynasty abdicated. Until then the royalty had spent the warmer months in Potsdam, not Berlin, and thus it was Potsdam where the ambitious monarchy came to display its achievements.

No one mastered the art of majestic self-presentation more virtuously than King Friedrich II, also known as Frederick the Great (1712–86). With his stylish sense of aesthetic and expressive architecture, the musically-talented king elevated the simple garrison town to the ranks of a glorious imperial residence. His Sanssouci Palace is one of Prussia's artistic highlights and a much-admired Rococo masterpiece.

A century before Frederick the Great entered the picture, the Great Elector Frederick William of Brandenburg (1620–88) had laid the foundations for Potsdam to become a princely domain. He chose the site on the previously insignificant Havel River to serve as his second residence near Berlin. The castle he built has recently been resurrected as a city palace. Potsdam will forever be associated with the Great Elector's Tolerance Edict of 1685, which made it possible for persecuted French Huguenots to settle in Brandenburg.

Potsdam was still a village when a Dutch friend of the Elector, Count Moritz von Nassau, had a vision that he shared with Frederick Wilhelm, which strongly influenced the future of Potsdam: "The whole island must become a paradise," he told the Elector. Generations of superb architects, garden designers and sculptors have helped ensure that through many different artistic ages this idea became reality.

Worthy of special note is the congenial cooperation between the master builder Karl Friedrich Schinkel and the landscape architect Peter Joseph Lenné. In the first half of the 19th century, under King Frederick William III (1770–1840) and Frederick William IV (1795–1861), Schinkel and Lenné

transformed the picturesque Potsdam landscape on the Havel River into a Prussian arcadia, a romantic ideal world. The ring of palaces and parks around the Jungfernsee Lake resembles a portrait of eternal bliss. This Prussian paradise became part of the UNESCO world culture heritage in 1990.

When the monarchy came to an end, this aristocratic resplendence was replaced by the glitz and glamour of the film industry. Over the last century the area of Babelsberg has come to embody a dream factory. It used to be famous UFA actors and actresses working in the film studios; today it is Hollywood stars who appear before the camera here.

Potsdam's fame, however, is not limited to its historic role as the Prussian royal seat of power or to glamorous filmmaking. It is also an important city of science. Illustrious names such as Nobel laureate Albert Einstein are also connected with what is today the state capital of Brandenburg. The Center for Climate Research in Potsdam contributes strongly to the city's internationally significant role in science.

This worthy past, which continued even after the Hohenzollern era ended, has continued to draw the powerful to Potsdam. Two important events in German history took place in Potsdam, representing both the beginning and the end of the National Socialist dictatorship: The "Day of Potsdam" on March 21, 1933, was an act of state that Adolf Hitler contrived to mark the continuity of Prussian-German history; the "Potsdam Conference," which took place in summer 1945, was a meeting held by the three victorious allies of World War II to discuss the future of Germany.

In addition to the many lovely palaces in Potsdam, of which Sanssouci is just one, the city also contains several charming areas and picturesque corners that beckon visitors to embark on a journey into the past. Its carefree, cheerful charm in combination with the flair of past nobility makes the former seat of royal power one of Germany's most livable and likable cities.

This special city guide presents the most important highlights of this city of palaces to ensure that your visit to Potsdam will be an exciting and unforgettable experience. Short texts provide everything you need to know about the individual sites. The vivid up-to-date photographs give an excellent impression of Potsdam's unique atmosphere. Addresses, opening hours and directions, a practical information section, a city map and public transportation map as well as two registers make it easy for you to plan the details of your journey through one of Europe's most magnificent cultural landscapes.

Altes Rathaus
Old City Hall

In other European cities, the city hall is often an expression of the pride and influence of its citizens. The Old City Hall in Potsdam, however, reflects the unlimited power that the Prussian majesties wielded over the city landscape. King Frederick II (1712–86) had the City Hall remodeled according to his own taste and at the expense of the state in 1753–55. He wanted the **Old Market Square** to radiate with the stately dignity of an historic capital. Jan Bouman the Elder and Carl Ludwig Hildebrandt modeled the magnificent facade on an unused design that the Italian building master Andrea Palladio had made for a palace in northern Italy. The tambour cupola, which housed a prison until 1875, is topped by a gilded Atlas carrying the weight of the globe on his shoulders.
Destroyed in World War II, the City Hall was rebuilt in 1963–66 with a facade that was true to the original. A new wing was added at the time, connecting the main building with the historic residential home on the corner of Brauerstrasse that had been built in 1750 according to plans by Frederick the Great's personal architect, Georg Wenzeslaus von Knobelsdorff. The building ensemble initially served as the "Hans Marwitza" cultural center.
In 2012 the **Potsdam Museum** established itself in the Old City Hall. Its collection of 250,000 artifacts on the city's history includes a document from 993 marking the establishment of Potsdam.

Potsdam Museum
Am Alten Markt 9
Tue–Fri 10am–5pm, Thu 10am–7pm, Sat/Sun 10am–6pm
Tel. 289 68 68; www.potsdam-museum.de

▷ Tram 91, 92, 93, 96, 98, 99 Alter Markt

Old Market Square: Old City Hall and Knobelsdorff building

On top of City Hall: Golden Atlas with globe

Modeled after the Romans: Old Market Square with City Hall and obelisk

1000 years of urban history: Potsdam Museum

(clockwise from top left)

Babelsberg, Schloss
Babelsberg Palace

It is a fairytale castle of Romanticism: The Babelsberg Palace rises above the Havel like a medieval fortress. The unusual career of the lord of the manor also seems out of a fairytale. Born as the second son, he initially had no claim to the throne, but he became King of Prussia after the death of his brother Frederick William IV – and later rose to become the ruler of the German Reich that was proclaimed in 1871.

The later Emperor William I (1797–1888) was still a prince when he built his summer residence in 1834. It was initially designed by Karl Friedrich Schinkel in the English Tudor style. But following the death of his father, King Frederick William III, and on account of his brother remaining childless, William unexpectedly became a contender for the crown in 1840, and no longer felt that the first neo-Gothic palace built on the European continent was stately enough. He had the architects Ludwig Persius and Johann Heinrich Strack enlarge the two-story brick building into a veritable castle with fortress-like tower in 1849. The ballroom in the octagonal center tower is a unique neo-Gothic gem.

The eccentric Prince Hermann von Pückler-Muskau was hired to rearrange the palace park grounds that had originally been designed by

Park Babelsberg 10
Currently under renovation. Call for opening hours:
Tel. 949 62 00; www.spsg.de

Flatow Tower
Park Babelsberg 12
May–Oct Sat/Sun 10am–6pm

▷ S 7 Babelsberg, transfer to Bus 616 Schloss Babelsberg

Like a medieval fortress: Babelsberg Palace

Once stood in Berlin: Court Arbor

In neo-Gothic style: Grand Banquet Hall

Designed by Prince Pückler: Babelsberg Palace Park

(clockwise from top left)

Peter Joseph Lenné. The famous landscape gardener transformed the Babelsberg scenery into a romantic park landscape with picturesque fountains, creeks and waterfalls and original flowerbed arrangements. The 40-meter high water fountain on the Havel River rises higher than the fountain in Park Sanssouci after which it was modeled.

The **Flatow Tower**, which was built between 1853 and 1856 by Johann Heinrich Strack is one of the attractions in the third-largest palace gardens in Potsdam. It was designed to resemble the medieval Eschenheimer Gate Tower in Frankfurt am Main. Used as a guesthouse by the royal couple, the tower today houses an exhibition on the history of the Babelsberg Park. The **Court Arbor**, an original from the Middle Ages, was built as a court of justice and extension to the old Berlin City Hall and was moved to Babelsberg in 1872. William I's wife, the later Empress Augusta (1811–90), had a penchant for English architecture, a fact best demonstrated by the **Little Palace** that was built on the bank of the Havel in the style of Tudor Gothic in 1843. Frederick III (1831–88) and his wife, the later Victoria (1840–1901) spent their honeymoon in this building in 1858. It is now a restaurant.

With a view of the Havel: pump station for palace park fountains

Seen from afar: Flatow Tower

Now a café: Small Palace

Between the Havel and Flatow Tower: Sailors' House

(clockwise from top left)

Bildergalerie
Picture Gallery

The Picture Gallery is one of the most magnificent painting collections in all of Europe. Frederick the Great had it built right next to his → **Sanssouci Palace**. The view of the long hall adorned with floors of yellow and white marble from antique quarries and elaborate gilded stucco makes every visitor wax poetic. No less impressive is the collection of works by Flemish and Italian artists, such as Michelangelo Merisi da Caravaggio, Pieter Brueghel the Elder, Peter Paul Rubens and Anthonis van Dyck.
The building, erected in 1764 by Johann Gottfried Büring, was quite unique at the time. Until then the nobility had presented their precious paintings inside their private palaces. Frederick II built the Picture Gallery for the explicit purpose of preserving his collection and presenting selected works to visitors. It is thus one of the oldest independent museum buildings in Germany.
The heads on the facade depict famous artists, such as Albrecht Dürer and Rubens. The Oranier Rondell, surrounded by marble busts of Dutch relatives of the House of Hohenzollern, lies in the Baroque **Dutch Gardens** in front of the Picture Gallery.

Im Park Sanssouci 4
May–Oct Tue–Sun 10am–5:30 pm
Tel. 969 42 00; www.spsg.de

▷ Bus X15, 695 Schloss Sanssouci

Dream in gold and marble: east wing of Picture Gallery

View from the Oranier Rondell: Frederick II's treasure chamber

Allegorical representation of science: sculpture in front of facade

(clockwise from above)

Brandenburger Straße
Brandenburger Strasse

The Brandenburger Strasse is a popular pedestrian zone in the historic center. It contains a large number of small, low-rise buildings, which is unusual for a bustling shopping mile. These modest structures were erected in 1734–38, when King Frederick William I (1688–1740) expanded the city of Potsdam for the second time during his reign. The stately shopping mall on the corner of Jägerstrasse stands out amidst the two-story buildings from the 18th century. The glass-covered atrium and art-nouveau glass roof on the first upper level deserve a special look.
The street runs in a straight line from the St. Peter and Paul Church on Bassinplatz to the **Brandenburg Gate** on Luisenplatz. Frederick II had the city gate erected in 1770–71 in the style of Roman triumphal arches to commemorate the Seven Years' War (1756–63). The facade facing the city was designed by Carl von Gontard; the side facing Luisenplatz was created by Georg Christian Unger.
The **St. Peter and Paul Church** was built a century later and also has an Italian precursor: The bell tower with it conical brick roof is modeled after the campanile of the San Zeno Church in Verona. The church's Byzantine-style interior is decorated with colorful mosaics.

St. Peter and Paul Church
Bassinplatz
Tue–Sat 4pm–6pm, Sat/Sun 12pm–5pm
www.peter-paul-kirche.de

▷ Tram 92, 96, Bus 638 Brandenburger Straße

At the eastern end of Brandenburger Strasse: St. Peter and Paul Church
Building landmark from 1905: department store
Popular meeting place: Luisenplatz in front of Brandenburg Gate
Colorful: imitation of Byzantine art in church hall
(clockwise from top left)

KARSTADT
KARSTADT

ROMAE VOLUNTATIS

Caputh
Caputh

The oldest palace in Potsdam stands in Caputh, a town on the southern bank of the Templin Lake. The **Caputh Palace** was built in 1671 under the Great Elector (1620–88) by his second wife, Dorothea von Holstein-Glücksburg (1636–89), as her country estate. Designed in the Italian-Dutch style, the house is a gem from the early Baroque area. The dining room, which was covered in 7,500 blue and white Dutch faience tiles in 1720, is particularly interesting. The famous Meeting of the Three Kings took place in the Caputh Palace in 1709. The first Prussian king, Frederick I, had invited the kings of Poland and Denmark, August II and Frederick IV, to join him here.

Albert Einstein (1879–1955) also enjoyed spending the summer months in Caputh. The physicist owned a simple wooden house near the lake, built in 1929, and he liked to invite artists and scientists to join him in informal conversation there. Sadly, he was only able to enjoy the idyllic surroundings for three summers: he immigrated to the United States in 1933. Today the **Einstein House** belongs to the Hebrew University of Jerusalem and is open to the public.

Caputh Palace
Strasse der Einheit 2
14548 Caputh
April–Oct Tue–Sun 10am–5:30pm, Nov–Mar Sat/Sun 10am–4pm
Tel. 033209/703 45; www.spsg.de

Einstein House
Am Waldrand 15–17
14584 Caputh
Apr–Oct Sat/Sun 10am–6pm
www.einsteinsommerhaus.de

▷ RB 23, Bus 607, Station Caputh Schwielowsee

Idyllic summer residence: Albert Einstein's hideaway

One-of-a-kind: tile-clad dining room of Caputh Palace

Early Baroque gem: oldest palace in Potsdam

From the time of the Great Elector: royal banquet hall

(clockwise from top left)

Cecilienhof, Schloss
Cecilienhof Palace

The Potsdam Conference, the historic meeting attended by the victors of World War II, took place in the palace in the **New Garden**, not far from the Jungfernsee Lake. Soviet leader Joseph Stalin, U.S. President Harry Truman and British Prime Minister Winston Churchill (later replaced by his successor Clement Attlee) convened at the Cecilienhof Palace from July 17 to August 2, 1945. This is where the "Big Three" sealed the postwar order of Europe, which led to the division of Germany and Europe into an East and a West.
The Soviet Union chose to host the conference in the palace in the New Garden – it was the newest and most comfortable of the Hohenzollern palaces. It was built in 1913–17 for the Crown Prince Wilhelm of Prussia (1882–1951) and his wife Cecilie of Mecklenburg-Schwerin (1886–1954). At the end of the monarchy in 1918, the couple continued to live here until they were forced to flee shortly before the end of World War II.
Architect Paul Schultze-Naumburg designed the palace to resemble a British Tudor-style country house. Decorative chimneys adorn the cottage, which contains 176 rooms. The large hall, living quarters of the heir to the imperial thrown, served as the Allies' conference hall in 1945. Visitors can view the round negotiating table as well as some of the private rooms of his excellency.

Im Neuen Garten 11
Apr–Oct Tue–Sun 10am–5:30pm, Nov/Dec Tue–Sun 10am–5pm, Jan–Mar Tue–Sun 10am–4:30pm
Tel. 969 42 00; www.spsg.de

▷ Bus 603 Schloss Cecilienhof

Youngest Hohenzollern palace: Cecilienhof Palace in New Garden

Now a restaurant: old dairy farm near palace

Where the Allies convened: meeting room of Potsdam Conference

(clockwise from above)

Charlottenhof, Schloss
Charlottenhof Palace

To help his son acquire his own palace, King Frederick William III gave the 30-year-old Crown Prince Frederick William (1795–1861) the Charlottenhof estate situated southwest of the Sanssouci Palace for Christmas in 1825. The building master Karl Friedrich Schinkel converted the manor house into a villa based on Roman patterns. The heir to the throne had architectural talent and contributed his own sketches. Together the two men created a jewel of Prussian Classicism. Schinkel also designed the ten interior rooms. The naturalist Alexander von Humboldt resided in the original tent room from 1835 to 1840.

An enchanting rose garden and sublime Poets Grove flank the smallest palace in Park → **Sanssouci**, lending the estate an intimate atmosphere. A bust of Elisabeth von Bayern (1801–73), who became Queen of Prussia after marrying Frederick William IV in 1840, rests on a column in the northern pond.

The **Roman Baths**, picturesque country houses designed jointly by Schinkel and the crown prince, are only a short walk from the palace. In cooperation with the building master Ludwig Persius, an imitation antique building ensemble was created which, like its Roman models, contains numerous sculptures and frescos.

Geschwister-Scholl-Strasse 34a
May–Oct Tue–Sun 10am–5:30pm
Tel. 969 42 00; www.spsg.de

Roman Baths
May–Oct Tue–Sun 10am–5:30pm

▷ Tram 91, 94, 98, Bus 605, 606 Schloss Charlottenhof

Modeled after antiquity: Schinkel's Charlottenhof Palace

Accommodations for Alexander von Humboldt: palace tent room

Attesting to the king's wanderlust: inner courtyard of Roman Baths

With jasper tub and marble statues: Caldarium in Roman Baths

(clockwise from top left)

Dampfmaschinenhaus (Moschee)
Steam Engine Building (Mosque)

This striking structure on the Neustädter Havelbucht, a bay of the Havel River, looks like an Ottoman mosque. In truth, however, it is a secular building. This oriental-looking architecture contains innovative technology from the era of the industrial revolution.
The Steam Engine Building was built in 1841–43 under the reign of Frederick William IV (1795–1861) so that the fanciful water displays in Park → **Sanssouci** could begin to spout water. The fountains had been created by Frederick II a century earlier. A two-cylinder machine with 82 horsepower began pumping water out of the Havel River and into the basin located 1,800 meters away in the → **Ruinenberg**. The Borsig company's most advanced machinery made it possible for water in the Great Fountain in front of the Sanssouci Palace vineyard to soar 38 meters into the air, just as Frederick the Great had intended.
The royal building master Ludwig Persius was given the task of creating a decorative structure to contain the noisy, smoking machinery that would fit in architecturally with Potsdam's dream world. He decided to disguise the unglamorous chimney as a minaret. Persius designed the machine room ornately, making references to the Moorish architecture of Mezquita von Córdoba and the Alhambra Fortress in Granada.

Breite Strasse 28
Only accessible during events
www.spsg.de

▷ Tram 91, 94, 98, Bus 605, 606 Feuerbachstraße

Resembling a mosque: Steam Engine Building on Havel Bay

Moorish architecture: view into engine room

Powerful technology: cogwheels from 1843

Artful iron construction: upper arcade

(clockwise from top left)

Filmmuseum
Film Museum

The Film Museum is simply a must for film buffs. Everything in the historic "Marstall," the Royal Stables of the → **City Palace**, revolves around the world of celluloid. The exhibition focuses on the history of the world-famous studios in the → **Babelsberg media center** that was founded over 100 years ago. From the legendary dream factories of UFA and DEFA up to the present: The Film Museum displays props, costumes, obsolete recording equipment and posters. It also presents old movies nearly every day in its cinema. A special highlight is the original 1920s cinema organ that was played to provide musical accompaniment during silent movies.
The Marstall, where the Film Museum is housed since 1981, was originally built as the City Palace Orangery in 1685. The building was converted into stables under Frederick William I. Its current appearance goes back to the reign of Frederick II. The sculpture of horses on the Attica, created by Friedrich Christian Glume the Younger, are particularly impressive.
The **Steuben Monument** lies behind the Marstall. General Frederick William von Steuben (1730–94), a native of Magdeburg, became a hero in the American War of Independence. He died in New York where a parade is held in his honor each year.

Breite Strasse 1A
Tue–Sun 10am–6pm
Tel. 271 81 12; www.filmmuseum-potsdam.de

▷ Tram 91, 92, 93, 96, 98, 99 Alter Markt/ Landtag

Former stables: Germany's oldest film museum

Meeting place for cineasts: museum cinema

In the limelight: stars und starlets

Playful presentation of movie history: museum exhibition

(clockwise from above)

FILMMUSEUM POTSDAM
FILM MUSEUM

Mimen & Masken

Freundschaftsinsel
Friendship Island

An island on the Havel River is one of the most beautiful green oases in Potsdam. The seven-hectare Friendship Island lies on the Lange Brücke, the long bridge between the main train station and the old town. The island was designed as a park in 1938–40, at which time the two gatehouses were also added. Behind them lies a diverse wildlife of blossoming bushes, more than 100,000 perennials and 35,000 different kinds of flowers. Information signs like the ones found in botanical gardens provide facts about the plants, some of which are quite exotic.
Friendship Island is a mix of three different decades: The 1930s, 1950s and 1970s. The colorful sea of flowers is a blooming homage to the garden expert Karl Foerster (1874–1970), who worked in Potsdam from 1910 until his death. Foerster, a perennial grower and garden poet, influenced the development of Friendship Island both before and after World War II. More than 200 perennials in the island park were grown by Foerster personally. In honor of the professor with the green thumb, a stainless steel monument was erected on Friendship Island in 1974.
Other attractions on the island include the water axis with its lilies and fountains, an exhibition pavilion and a café. Special events are held on the outdoor stage.

Lange Brücke
Open until dusk
www.freundschaftsinsel-potsdam.de

▷ Tram 91, 92, 93, 96, 98, 99 Lange Brücke

Paradise: flora on Friendship Island

Balancing act: paddling upright on "Alte Fahrt" waterway

Waiting for a catch: heron

Honoring the perennial grower: monument to Karl Foerster

(clockwise from above)

Friedenskirche und Marlygarten
Church of Peace and Marly Gardens

Two Prussian kings and one German emperor found their final resting place here: The Church of Peace was the first house of prayer in → **Sanssouci**, erected 100 years after completion of the Sanssouci palace. Frederick William IV (1795–1861) and his wife Elisabeth of Bavaria (1801–73), who commissioned the structure, are buried in the crypt inside the church, which was built in 1845–56 and modeled after the early Christian churches built in Rome. There is a precious golden mosaic in the altar room. This medieval artwork from the year 1108 came from the torn-down Church San Cipriano on the island of Murano near Venice.
A mausoleum was created for Emperor Frederick III (1831–88) in the cloister-like ensemble of the Church of Peace in which the sarcophagus of his British wife Victoria (1840–1901) also lies. The mausoleum also contains other members of the Hohenzollern family, including King Frederick William I (1688–1740), who was added in 1991. The neo-Baroque cupola was designed by Julius Carl Raschdorff, who was also the architect of the Berlin Cathedral.
The decorative Marly Gardens, west of the church, served as a kitchen garden for the crown before they were redesigned into a landscape garden in 1847.
The **Triumphal Gate** of terracotta reliefs near Weinbergstrasse was built by Frederick William IV in 1850 to idealize Prussia's history.

Am Grünen Gitter 3
Church is open from Mar 15 to Oct 15
Tel. 969 42 00; www.spsg.de

▷ Bus X15, 614 Friedenskirche

From the Middle Ages: mosaic in altar room of Church of Peace

Sublime: basilica of Church of Peace and mausoleum (right)

Remembering Prussia's power: Triumphal Gate at vineyard hill

Amidst an artfully-arranged bed: flower goddess Flora in Marly Gardens

(clockwise from top left)

FRIEDRICH WILHELM IV. K. P.
HAT DIES THOR ZU ERBAUEN BEFOHLEN HUNDERT UND SECHS JAHRE
NACH DER GRÜNDUNG VON SANS-SOUCI
MDCCCLI

Garnisonkirche
Garrison Church

The Garrison Church was once a landmark and the tallest structure in Potsdam. This house of prayer with it 89-meter-high church spire was also a symbol of the Prussian military state. It was built by the soldier king Frederick William (1688–1740) in 1730 where it could be seen from the → **City Palace** on Breite Strasse. After his death, the ruler was buried here and joined by Frederick II, his heir to the throne, in 1786. The church became a cult site for supporters of the Prussian throne.
It was in this church on March 21, 1933, in celebration of the newly elected parliament, that the National Socialists presented Hitler rubbing shoulders with the elite of the lost German empire. This historic event, known as the "Day of Potsdam," became a stigma, which is why the GDR government had the church torn down in 1968. Plans to rebuild the church, a project that has been highly controversial, are based on the original designs by the Prussian architect Johann Philipp Gerlach. Construction is scheduled to begin in 2018 and will begin with the reconstruction of the church spire. The Garrison Church's legendary 40-voice tower bells resound again in the nearby park, which is named **Plantage** in reference to its previous function as a plantation. Georg Christian Unger's magnificent building facade of 1734 has also survived. It was once part of the **Long Stables**, a riding hall from 1780 that was destroyed in World War II.

Exhibition on the history of the Garrison Church
Nagelkreuzkapelle
Breite Strasse 7
Tue–Sun 11am–5pm
Tel. 201 18 30; www.garnisonkirche-potsdam.de

▷ Bus X15, 606, 580 Schloßstraße

Recast: Renowned Glockenspiel of Garrison Church

Soon to return to the church spire: weather vane with Prussian insignia

Just a facade: magnificent front of Long Stables

(clockwise from above)

Gedenkstätte Leistikowstraße
Leistikowstrasse Memorial

Potsdam's military history also includes the 50 years that the city served as a garrison town of the Soviet Army. The walled-in **Military Town No. 7** on the outskirts of Nauen was a feared site of the Cold War. The Soviet secret service occupied more than 100 buildings here at the end of World War II. The headquarters of its German counterintelligence division took over the residence of the Kaiserin-Augusta-Stiftung in the New Gardens. The complex also contained a remand prison that was established in the parish house on Leistikowstrasse. The Leistikowstrasse Memorial and Meeting Place that opened in 2009 documents the cruel punishment and suffering inflicted on prisoners by the secret service. Germans and people of many other nationalities were interrogated and mistreated in this prison until 1955. After that only Soviet citizens were held here. Today this authentic site of the Cold War is open to the public.
The Russian troops withdrew from Potsdam in 1994 and the "forbidden city" was accessible to everyone again by April 1995. A history trail runs through what is today a tranquil and elegant residential neighborhood. Many reminders of the postwar era are marked by information signs between Grosse Weinmeisterstrasse and Am Neuen Garten.

Leistikowstrasse 1
Apr–Oct Tue–Sun 2pm–6pm, Nov–Mar Tue–Sun 1pm–5pm
Tel. 201 15 40, www.gedenkstaette-leistikowstrasse.de

▷ Tram 92, 96 Puschkinallee, Bus 603 Persiusstraße

Monument: former KGB prison on Leistikowstrasse (right)

Documenting history: sanitary facilities in prison

Informative: history trail through former Military Town No. 7

Commemorating painful fates: Leistikowstrasse Memorial

(clockwise from top left)

Glienicke, Schloss
Glienicke Palace

Although the Glienicke Palace and its connecting park are situated outside the city limits in Berlin, they belong to the cultural landscape of Potsdam. The lakeside estate on the Jungfernsee was created for Prince Charles (1801–83), the third son of King Frederick William III and Queen Luise. The Prussian luminaries Karl Friedrich Schinkel and Peter Joseph Lenné designed a work of art of exceptional beauty. In 1825–27 the architect Schinkel converted a manor house on the edge of → **Klein Glienicke** that had once belonged to German Chancellor Karl August Fürst von Hardenberg into a palace for the prince. The scenery in front of the palace, which resembled an Italian villa, is dominated by the splendid Lions Fountain of 1838. The **Casino** on the bank of the Havel offers a glorious view across the Jungfernsee Lake. Schinkel's original creations include the **Grosse Neugierde** – which translates literally as "large curiosity" – a rotunda that was built in 1835 as a look-out point in the style of Greek Antiquity. The English-style palace gardens were designed by Lenné as pleasure grounds with numerous antique and contemporary works of art grouped together picturesquely.
The **Glienicke Bridge** connects the palace park with Potsdam. The United States and Soviet Union exchanged spies on this bridge during the Cold War.

Königstrasse 36
14109 Berlin
Apr–Oct Tue–Sun 10am–5:30pm, Nov/Dec Sat/Sun 10am–5pm, Mar Sat/Sun 10am–4pm
Tel. 969 42 00; www.spsg.de

▷ Tram 93 Glienicker Brücke, transfer to Bus 316 Schloss Glienicke

Mediterranean flair: Lions Fountain in front of Glienicke Palace

Also by Schinkel: Casino in Glienicke Park

Connecting Potsdam and Berlin: Glienicke Bridge

Lookout point in the classical style: Grosse Neugierde

(clockwise from above)

HBPG
House of Branden-burg-Prussian History

Potsdam is the capital of a German state with a moving history: Brandenburg has existed for nearly 900 years. In 1157, Albrecht the Bear was appointed margrave of the area situated east of the German Reich. The House of Brandenburg and Prussian History presents the changes and developments in this region from the Middle Ages through the glorious era of Prussia under the reign of the Hohenzollern family up to the 20th century.

The saddle of Elector Joachim II (1505–71), who avowed himself to Luther's reformed Christianity, is shown in the permanent exhibition. It also shows the death mask of the popular Prussian Queen Luise, who died in 1810 at the young age of 34. A large model of Potsdam replicates how the city looked in 1912. There is also a very informative collection on the 1920s when Potsdam became a popular day-trip destination for Berliners.

The House of Brandenburg and Prussian History is located in the former Royal Carriage Stables which were built in 1787–90. The crown's coach horses were kept in this complex on **New Market Square** until 1918. There is an impressive sculptural group above the entrance portal that depicts Frederick the Great's personal coachman steering a four-horse carriage.

Am Neuen Markt 9
Tue–Thu 10am–5pm, Fri–Sun 10am–6pm
Tel. 620 85 50; www.hbpg.de

▷ Tram 91, 92, 93, 96, 98, 99 Alter Markt/Landtag

City model in House of Branden-burg-Prussian History: Potsdam in 1912

Overlooking the entrance: Frederick's personal coachman with four-horse carriage

Environmentally friendly: carriages from glorious era of Prussia

In the former Royal Carriage Stables: museum on Brandenburg history

(clockwise from top left)

Havel
Havel

Brandenburg's capital is surrounded on all sides by water, which is why it is often referred to as "Potsdam Island." This situation is created by the Havel River, which runs north to south through the historic city center before curving northward at the southern edge of the city. The Sacrow Paretz Canal on the north tip of the city creates a short-cut to the Havel's circuitous route around the city.

In Potsdam, Brandenburg's longest river merges into the Elbe River, creating a chain of lakes: Jungfernsee, Tiefer See, Templiner See and Schwielowsee. Four more lakes are situated directly in the city: Heiliger See, Bornsteder See, Sacrower See and Griebnitzsee.

These many waterways make Potsdam increasingly attractive to its residents and visitors. Water sports are very popular here. The oarsmen and canoers of Potsdam have been among the best athletes in the world for decades.

The abundance of water has also left its mark on the historic center. The central green areas – Bassinplatz, Platz der Einheit and Plantage – exist because the swampy soil was not suitable for building houses.

Excursion boats like the "Weisse Flotte" make it possible to see Potsdam from its most attractive side: from the water.

Weisse Flotte Potsdam
Lange Brücke 6
Tel. 275 92 10 (Schedule: Tel. 275 92 33)
www.schifffahrt-in-potsdam.de

▷ Tram 91, 92, 93, 96, 98, 99 Lange Brücke/Alter Markt

With the Flatow Tower: Havel River at Babelsberg Park

Exploring Potsdam by water: pleasure boat on Havel River

Where boats are a part of the cityscape: Potsdam water paradise

Bringing fresh fish to the table: fisher on Havel River

(clockwise from top left)

Holländisches Viertel
Dutch Quarter

Life like in Holland. Soldier King Frederick William I (1688–1740) hoped that this original idea would attract well-trained tradesmen from Holland to Potsdam. In 1732 he ordered a neighborhood to be built in the Dutch style. By 1742, 134 brick houses with a back garden were completed on both sides of today's Mittel- and Benkertstrasse. Building master Jan Bouman the Elder, who came from Holland, was in charge of the project. But "Little Amsterdam" didn't fill its intended purpose: few artisans from the wealthy neighboring country resettled there. Today this attractive neighborhood that spans four streets is home to many stylish restaurants and upscale shops. The **Jan Bouman House**, a typical gable house from 1735, is open to the public. It gives an impression of what daily life was like here in the 18th century and provides information on the history of this unique building ensemble. A famous Prussian tailor is also here at Mittelstrasse 3: This is where in 1906 the "Captain of Köpenick," Schuster Wilhelm Voigt, purchased the uniform that he wore when he arrested the mayor of Köpenick and confiscated the city treasury.
The **Nauen Gate** on the edge of the Dutch Quarter is quite unusual. It was erected in 1755 by court architect Johann Gottfried Büring on the basis of a design by Frederick II and is the first neo-Gothic structure in Prussia. The arched opening through the middle was added in 1867.

Jan Bouman Haus
Mittelstrasse 8
Mon–Fri 1pm–6pm, Sat/Sun 11am–6pm
Tel. 280 37 73, www.jan-bouman-haus.de

▷ Tram 92, 96, Bus 638 Nauener Tor

Lined up: brick gable house in Dutch Quarter
On the edge of Little Amsterdam: Nauen Gate
From above: Nauen Gate and Dutch Quarter (right)
Modestly furnished: original cooking niche in Jan Bouman House
(clockwise from top left)

Jagdschloss Stern
Stern Hunting Lodge

The Stern Hunting Lodge on the eastern edge of the city is the smallest of the Potsdam palaces. It is also the only palace that the frugal King Frederick William I (1688–1740) built during the 27 years of his reign.
The modest brick structure recalls the soldier king's great passion for hunting. Three hundred years ago, the developed area we see today was called Parforceheide and was a dense woodland. The king had some 100 square meters fenced in so it could be used as hunting grounds. To facilitate the popular hunting style known as coursing, pathways were established through the forest that converge in a star-like formation at a central point.
The palace, designed to resemble a Dutch townhouse, was built for the king at this remote hunting spot in 1730–32. The structure designed by the architect Pierre de Gayette also served as a model for the → **Dutch Quarter** that was being planned in Potsdam.
The king put the antlers of his favorite deer on display in the Baroque hall inside the house. The simple furnishings within the royal chambers reflect Frederick William I's resolute character as a man who preferred the simple, rustic lifestyle.

Jagdhausstrasse 1A
Viewings during events
Tel. 58 29 11 37; www.jagdschloss-stern.de

▷ Tram 92, 96 Gaußstraße, Bus 601, 694 Jagdhausstraße

Smallest Hohenzollern palace: Soldier King's Stern Hunting Lodge

Catering to the guests' well-being: palace kitchen

Room for the royal hunting society: Large Hall

Recalling Frederick William I's passion for hunting: antler trophy

(clockwise from top left)

Kaiserbahnhof
Emperor's Station

Emperor Wilhelm II (1859–1941) was known as the restless "traveling emperor." He was on the road in the German Reich and abroad for more than half the year, traveling in wooden trains made especially for him. His chroniclers have counted 199 travel days in the year 1894 alone.

William II resided during the summer months in the → **New Palace** and used the "Wildpark," a nearby railway stop called Potsdam Park Sanssouci today. In 1909 a 90-meter-long, separate station hall for the "emperor's track" was built for His Majesty. Court architect Ernst Eberhard von Ihne designed the royal court station in the English cottage style.

U.S. President Theodor Roosevelt was the first state guest to arrive at the Emperor's Station. The Russian Czar Nicholas II was given a grand reception in November 1910. After the November Revolution and the end of the monarchy in 1918, 59 freight cars were needed to bring the royal couple to exile in Holland and transport their possessions to Doorn.

When Empress Augusta Victoria died, her coffin was brought to this station on April 19, 1921 and buried in the antique temple near the New Palace. The funeral procession was followed by 200,000 spectators.

The German Railway Academy has used the Emperor's Station since May 2005. One of the thirty royal railway cars is on display on Track 1.

Am Neuen Palais 1
Station Park Sanssouci

▷ RE 1, RB 20, Bus X5, 605, 606, 695 Park Sanssouci

With its own railway platform hall: Emperor's Station of Wilhelm II

Standing on Track 1: royal railway car

Where guests of state were greeted until 1918: reception hall at Emperor's Station

(clockwise from above)

Park Sanssouci

Kiezstraße
Kiezstrasse

The Kiezstrasse is in one of the oldest sections of the city, an area that has retained some of its flair from the era of Frederick the Great (1712–86). The neighborhood was established in the 13th century as a Slavic fishermen's settlement and wasn't incorporated into Potsdam until 1722. Frederick II was responsible for the new buildings that we see on Kiezstrasse today. The architects Georg Christian Unger and Rudolf Heinrich Richter decorated the facades of these residential homes with fine Rococo ornamentation.
Chestnut trees were planted on the center promenade in the mid-19th century. The former building of the **Loge Minerva** (Kiezstrasse 10) also goes back to this time. The men's society, whose members were mostly affiliates of the royal household and the nobility, was founded after the Seven Years' War in 1768.
Breite Strasse, which forms the neighborhood's northern border, was the grand boulevard of Potsdam. The townhouses were adorned with elaborate facades on the request of Frederick II. The **Hiller-Brandtsche buildings** from 1769 are rather extravagant examples. Unger modeled the twin house on the corner of Dortustrasse after the British architect Inigo Jone's 1619 design of the Whitehall Palace in London. The **Museum of Natural History** stands catty-corner, housed in the former Zauche house of nobility from 1770.

Naturkundemuseum
Breite Strasse 13
Tue–Sun 9am–5pm
Tel. 289 67 07, www.naturkundemuseum-potsdam.de

▷ Bus X15, 606, 580 Naturkundemuseum

Finest facade ornamentation: Rococo decor on Kiezstrasse

Extravagant front: Hiller-Brandtsche buildings on Breite Strasse

Perfect for a stroll: center promenade of Kiezstrasse

Former house of nobility: Museum of Natural History on Breite Strasse

(clockwise from top left)

Klein Glienicke
Klein Glienicke

When visiting Potsdam, one need not travel far to make a brief interlude into Switzerland. It suffices to pay a visit to the area of Klein Glienicke where **Swiss Houses** were erected along the Bäke Canal to resemble Tirol farmhouses. Prince Charles of Prussia (1801–83) had the idea for this dreamy alpine panorama. He wanted to establish an alpine village as a connection between his "Italian" Glienicke Palace and his brother William's "Nordic" Babelsberg Palace. In 1863–66 Ferdinand von Arnim erected ten richly adorned residential houses with faux wooden walls made of stone. When Germany was divided from 1961–89, Klein Glienicke, known as the "appendix of the GDR," jutted into the West Berlin district of Zehlendorf and was almost completely surrounded by the Berlin Wall. As a consequence, many of the alpine houses were leveled during this time.
The **chapel** within these idyllic surroundings is an architectural treasure. This little church with its picturesque design of red and green glazed bricks was built in 1880–81 by Reinhold Persius. The **Glienicke Hunting Lodge**, which lies within the Berlin city limits on the western edge of Potsdam, is also an interesting structure. It was built in 1682–93 for the Great Elector and remodeled with Baroque forms under Prince Charles in 1860–62.

Klein Glienicke Chapel
Wilhelm-Leuschner Strasse 1a
To book tours: Tel. 70 57 94;
www.klein-glienicker-kapelle.de

▷ Tram 93, transfer to Bus 316 Schloss Glienicke or Bus 616 Schloss Babelsberg

Idyllic alpine landscape: Swiss house in Klein Glienicke

Picturesque: small chapel from the 19th century

Built in 1863–66: Tirol farmhouse on Prussian soil

Palace for Prince Charles: Glienicke Hunting Lodge

(clockwise from top left)

Krongut Bornstedt
Bornstedt Crown Estate

The Bornstedt Crown Estate acquired its current form as part of the large-scale renovation plans for Potsdam's surrounding area, designed by the royal garden director Peter Joseph Lenné in 1833. The monarchy acquired the former manor north of Sanssouci in 1841 and had it remodeled in the Italian style in 1846–48. The ensemble with the manor house, which was designed by the Prussian court building officer Johann Heinrich Haeberlin, represented a model farm of Prussian agriculture. Today it is a popular destination for daytrips, with elegant restaurants, a brewery, celebrations, concerts, markets and the **Potsdamer Zinnfiguren Museum**, a collection of tin figures. Once a month the "Langen Kerls," the very tall soldiers of the king's personal regiment, march across the estate grounds.

The **Bornstedt village church** stands across from the estate and was designed with Italian-style forms by the building master Friedrich August Stüler in 1855–56. Many historical figures from the Prussian aristocracy and middle-class are buried in the church cemetery. The **Sello Cemetery** is also the final resting place of the court gardener Emil Sello (1816–93), who designed the estate gardens in 1875; the superb landscape planner Lenné (1789–1866), who was active in Potsdam for a half century beginning in 1816; and the architect Ludwig Persius (1803–45).

Ribbeckstrasse 6/7
Tel. 55 06 50; www.krongut-bornstedt.de

Potsdamer Zinnfiguren Museum
Open daily 11am–6pm

▷ Tram 92 Kirschallee, Bus 614 Ribbeckstraße

With welcoming cafés and breweries: Bornstedt Crown Estate

Reminiscent of Tuscany: bold tower of the crown estate

Resting place of famous Prussians: Sello Cemetery

Work of Stüler: Bornstedt village church

(clockwise from top left)

Lindenstraße
Lindenstrasse

Sometimes the attractive building facades in Potsdam are a reflection not of history's highlights, but of its dark side. There are several examples of this on Lindenstrasse. The **Large Military Orphanage** on the corner of Breite Strasse was built by King Frederick William I in 1722–24 as a care facility for the children of fallen, deceased or impoverished soldiers. Frederick II had the building remodeled into something resembling a palace in 1771–78 following plans by Carl von Gontard. As a result of Frederick's many military campaigns during the Seven Years' War, homes like this were needed for as many as 2,500 orphans. Nearby, on Lindenstrasse 25, stands the tastefully decorated **Lazarette for the Royal Regiment**, erected during the same period by Georg Christian Unger. The Lindenstrasse is lined with Baroque **military barracks** built under Frederick the Great and used at one time as housing for married soldiers.

The **Old Guardhouse** on the intersection of Lindenstrasse and Charlottenstrasse was a "gift" from Frederick William II to his regiment, called "Prince of Prussia." The classical structure from 1797 replaced the gate, which had been built under the Frederick William I. The "soldier king" had a wall built around Potsdam to stop smuggling and military deserters. The Old Guardhouse also served at one time as a prison.

For a long time a political prison was hidden behind the stately facade of the Grand Dutch

Lindenstrasse Memorial
Lindenstrasse 54
Tue–Sun 10am–pm
Tel. 289 61 12, www.gedenkstaette-lindenstrasse.de

▷ Tram 91, 94, 98, Bus 695, 605 Dortustraße

Old Potsdam's largest building complex: military orphanage

Now an apartment house: military hospital on Lindenstrasse

Potsdam's oldest city gate: Jägertor

From the time of Frederick William II: Old Guardhouse on Charlottenstrasse

(clockwise from top left)

House at Lindenstrasse 54/55. Built in 1733–37 under the soldier king as a city palace for the commander of his personal guard, the building was used during the Nazi era as a remand prison for regime opponents. After the war the Soviet secret service took over the prison and operated it until 1953, after which it was used by the East German Ministry for State Security in the GDR (Stasi). Today it houses the **Lindenstrasse Memorial**, which documents political persecution under the Nazis and in the GDR. The **Jägertor**, erected in 1733 on the northern end of Lindenstrasse, is the oldest surviving city gate in Potsdam. It was once part of the city wall, which was designed to stop goods from being smuggled and soldiers from deserting. The Baroque figures on the gate depict a hunting scene and also convey the military function of the structure.

Remembering political persecution during two dictatorships: Lindenstrasse Memorial

Also known as "Linden Hotel": cell wing in remand prison

Serving as a prison after 1817: building complex on Lindenstrasse

Hiding behind the attractive facade of a city palace: cells for regime opponents

World behind bars: outdoor cell

(clockwise from top left)

Marmorpalais
Marble Palace

The **New Garden** and Marble Palace were the private realm of King Frederick William II (1744–97). The nephew and heir to the throne of Frederick II was known above all as a jovial ladies' man. His liaison with his first love and mistress, the beautiful Wilhelmine Encke (1753–1820), is legendary.

The dissolute monarch, however, showed good taste in architecture. His hideaway on Heiliger See Lake helped establish new stylistic trends throughout Prussia. The king entrusted the building of his Marble Palace in 1787 to the experienced Baroque architect Carl von Gontard. He also summoned the assistance of Carl Gotthard Langhans, a pioneer of Classicism, who was erecting the Brandenburg Gate in Berlin at the time.

The name of the summer palace comes from the elaborate use of Silesian marble on the early classical facade. The belvedere on the roof, which offers a lovely view of Peacock Island – just a boat ride away – recalls the Old City Hall. Two low level side wings were added to the main structure in 1797.

The delightful scenery around the lakeside Marble Palace represented a new design idea for royal parks. In the New Garden, the innovative landscape architect Johann August Eyserbeck created a "poetic landscape imagery" based on the English model. The second largest park grounds in Potsdam contains atmospheric

Im Neuen Garten 10
May–Oct Tue–Sun 10am–6pm, Nov–Mar Sat/Sun 10am–4pm, April Sat/Sun 10am–6pm
Tel. 969 42 00; www.spsg.de

▷ Bus 603 Am Neuen Garten/Große Weinmeisterstraße

One of the loveliest rooms in the Marble Palace: Oval Hall

Exotic: Oriental Cabinet

Dignified: concert and ballroom on the palace's lakeside

Perfect setting: Marble Palace on bank of Heiliger See lake

(clockwise from top left)

scenery and structures whose true purpose remains concealed and in some cases reflect the king's membership in a secret masonry lodge: The **Pyramid** served as an ice house for cold storage; the Roman **Temple Ruins** on the bank of the lake were actually a kitchen; the **Orangery** with Egyptian decoration was used as a concert hall. The **Gothic Library** (1792–94) at the tip of the park, designed by Langhans, contained two levels of books from Frederick William II's collection – including important works of German literature that had been vilified by his uncle.
Frederick the Great's nephew died in his Marble Palace in 1797. Twenty years later Joseph Lenné pepped up the gardens. A century later the → **Cecilienhof**, the last palace of the Hohenzollern family, was built in the New Garden.

Contained the royal collection of classical literature: Gothic library

In the New Garden: Frederick William II's early classical palace

Shaped like the pyramids: cold storage

Only looks like ruins: palace kitchen

Behind flowery garden grounds: Orangery

(clockwise from top left)

Matrosenstation Kongsnæs

Sailors' Station Kongsnæs

The Jungfernsee Lake is not a Norwegian fjord, but it does provide a view of a magnificent Norwegian-style log cabin. Potsdam's newest attraction goes back to Emperor William II (1859–1941), who was passionate about sailing. The emperor had an exotic structure erected to serve as the court docking area near the **New Garden**: It is a majestic waiting hall, called "Ventehalle," and built in the style of traditional Scandinavian block houses.
Before he ascended to the throne in 1888, William II traveled to Norway and took a liking to the country's typical log cabins with their skillful carvings. The dragon heads on the rooftop ridge are found on these Nordic buildings going as far back as the Middle Ages.
The royal house commissioned the Norwegian building master Holm Hansen Munthe, a specialist of old Norwegian architecture, to build the Royal Sailors' Station. The "Ventehalle on the Kongsnæs," built on the headland in 1893–95, burned down in World War II.
This sweet little treasure was reconstructed on the historic foundations and reopened in 2018 as a restaurant catering to tourists. The wooden portal is also a replica.

Schwanenallee 7
www.matrosenstation.de

▷ Tram 93 Glienicker Brücke

Returned: artful log cabin built on Emperor Wilhelm II's request

Kongsnæs: Norwegian name of the house emblazoned on wooden portal

Magnificent view: partly open wooden house on Jungfernsee lake

Scandinavian artistry: detail in reconstructed "Ventehalle"

(clockwise from top left)

Medienstadt Babelsberg

Babelsberg Media Center

The Babelsberg dream factory has written more than 100 years of film history: from the golden age of the UFA to the cinematic achievements of the DEFA up to the internationally acclaimed **Studio Babelsberg**. Countless movie classics were created in this district east of the city center. The first movie was filmed here in February 1912; in 1921 the legendary UFA Company (Universum-Film-Aktiengesellschaft) moved to Babelsberg, and five years later it built the largest film studio in Europe – today's **Marlene-Dietrich-Halle** on Billy-Wilder-Platz. The glamorous film city became a tool of propaganda during the Nazi dictatorship; after the war, in 1948, the newly founded DEFA began making films on the studio grounds. By 1989 more than 1300 feature and television films had been produced here. Since the turn of the millennium, the largest studio complex in Europe has become extremely popular, especially among Hollywood stars.

Filmpark Babelsberg is a great tourist attraction in Potsdam, providing visitors with a behind-the-scenes peak into filmmaking. Spectacular shows with breathtaking stunts are just one of the attractions on the open-air grounds. There is also a 4D and XD cinema.

Filmpark Babelsberg
Grossbeerenstrasse 200
Apr–Sept 10am–6pm, Oct 10am–5pm
Tel. 721 23 45 (tickets), 721 27 50 (info-hotline);
www.filmpark-babelsberg.de

Studio Babelsberg
August-Bebel-Strasse 26
The grounds are publicly accessible; for studio tours call: Tel. 721 21 32; www.studiobabelsberg.com

▷ Bus 601, 618, 619, 690 Filmpark

Wrote film history as UFA and DEFA: Studio Babelsberg

From "Jim Knopf and the Engine Driver": movie set in Babelsberg film park

Animal fun: dog in front of the camera

Thrilling the audience: stunt shows in film park

(clockwise from top left)

Museum Barberini
Barberini Museum

The Barberini Museum is Potsdam's newest art temple. The Baroque palace opened to the public in early 2017, presenting first-class exhibitions of works by internally acclaimed artists and sculptors. The museum's holdings are predominantly from the Hasso Plattner Collection. It is thanks to Plattner, a German businessman, that the Barberini Palace was rebuilt on the **Old Market Square**. The original building, destroyed in World War II, was erected under Frederick the Great (1712–86) in 1771/72. Building master Carl von Gontard modeled his design for the structure after the Roman Palazzo Barberini – a masterpiece of Carlo Maderno (1625–33). Gontard was fulfilling a wish of the Prussian king to design the Old Market Square with the Potsdam → **City Palace** in the style of a decorative Roman-Baroque plaza. The → **Old City Hall** and the first → **St. Nicholas Church** had already been built following Italian models in 1753. The marble obelisk on the Old Market Square also finds its precursors among the Baroque plazas of the Eternal City.
In 1845–49 building master Ludwig Persius added two side wings to the Barberini Palace. The reconstructed city palace, along with the neighboring replicated facades at Humboldtstrasse 3 and 4 (modeled after the Palazzo Pompej and Palazzo Chiericati), complete the Roman cityscape of the Frederick period.

Humboldtstrasse 5–6
Wed–Mon 10am–7pm, on the 1st Thursday in the month 10am–9pm
Tel. 236 01 44 99; www.museum-barberini.com

▷ Tram 91, 92, 93, 96, 98, 99 Alter Markt

Art palace: Museum Barberini opened on Old Market Square in 2017

Sculpture in the museum courtyard: "Century Step" by Wolfgang Mattheuer

First-class paintings: exhibit room in the museum

Replica: Old Potsdam with Barberini Palace on "Alte Fahrt" waterway

(clockwise from top left)

Neue Orangerie
New Orangery

The New Orangery marks the highpoint of the busy building activity in Potsdam under Frederick William IV (1795–1861). The "Romantic on the Throne" was the last monarch to influence the appearance of the royal city through the construction of several new buildings. He was inspired by his last trip to Italy in 1828, during which the artistically talented king made sketches of structures that he felt could be used to bring an Italian flair to the Havel. The New Orangery combines elements from the Villa Medici in Rome and the Uffizi in Florence. Situated on the hill in Park → **Sanssouci**, its elevated position reinforces the monumental quality of the 300-meter-long structure. The design, created by the king and Ludwig Persius and Friedrich August Stüler, was completed in 1851–64 by architect Ludwig Ferdinand Hesse. The Raphael Hall at the center of the complex displays 47 copies of paintings by the Italian Renaissance artist Raphael. The marble sculpture on the large terrace in front of the entrance portrays Frederick William IV.
West of the Orangery, a majestic pathway leads from the **Dragon House**, which resembles a Chinese pagoda, to the **Belvedere** on the Klausberg, both legacies of Frederick II.

An der Orangerie 3–5
April Sat/Sun 10am–6pm, May–Oct Tue–Sun 10am–6pm
Tel. 969 42 00; www.spsg.de

Restaurant and Café Drachenhaus
Maulbeerallee 4
Apr–Oct open daily 11am–8pm, Nov–Mar Tue–Sun 12pm–6pm
Tel. 505 38 08; www.drachenhaus.de

▷ Bus 695 Orangerie

Modeled after Renaissance buildings: New Orangery

Looking to Park Sanssouci: Frederick William IV

Following Chinese fashion: Dragon House

With a view to the distance: Belvedere on the Klausberg

(clockwise from above)

Neuer Markt
New Market Square

The historical cityscape from the era of Frederick II has survived almost entirely intact on New Market Square. To ensure that the harmonious ensemble of Baroque townhouses remain undisturbed, a reconstructed facade was added to a new structure built on the single empty lot left behind by the war. The new building is visible from behind the historicized front of the **Bürgerpalais** (Am Neuen Markt 5).
The most famous resident of the New Market Square was the nephew and successor to Frederick II, the later Frederick William II (1744–97). The prince lived at Am Neuen Markt 1 from 1764 until his ascension to the throne in 1786. The **Crown Prince Palace**, also called the Cabinet House, was the birthplace of another heir apparent: the later King Frederick William III entered the world at this site in 1770.
In 1714 the New Market Square was selected as the site of the **Royal Carriage Stables** because of its close proximity to the City Palace. The early classical facade was added to the complex at Am Neuen Markt 9 in 1787–89. The stables building now contains the → **House of Brandenburg-Prussian History**.
The **Ratswaage** (council scales) building was the last structure added to the center of the square in 1836. The preserved scale plate, imbedded into the cobblestones, continued to be used until well into the 1970s.

Am Neuen Markt

▷ Tram 91, 92, 93, 96, 98, 99 Alter Markt/ Landtag

Quintessential Old Potsdam: New Market Square with Ratswaage

Nursery of two heir apparents: Crown Prince Palace

Hiding behind a new building: Facade of Bürgerpalais

(clockwise from above)

Neues Palais
New Palace

The greatest palace complex in Prussia is not situated in an urban setting but instead nestled in nature on the western edge of the → **Sanssouci Park**. Frederick II (1712–86) built the New Palace to demonstrate to the world that through the Seven Years' War (1756–63) Prussia had acquired the status of a major power in Europe. Together with the monumental Communs, the New Palace forms a majestic ensemble on the scale of the Versailles Palace in Paris and the Schönbrunn Palace in Vienna.

The Communs originally contained utility rooms and accommodations for servants and guests. Today it houses several institutes and administration offices of the Potsdam University.

The New Palace, built in 1763–69, primarily under the supervision of building master Carl von Gontard, first served as a guesthouse with additional apartments for the royal family. Frederick the Great used the side wings on the south side. The palace halls radiate a courtly pomp that even the king found to be "ostentatious." The marble hall, the most impressive of the preserved Hohenzollern Palace banquet halls, represents the highpoint. The Grotto Hall, decorated with 250,000 shells, is also quite unique. Another rarity is the Hall of the Royal Palace Theater, where performances are held again today. The chambers of Frederick II are a masterpiece of Frederick-era Rococo.

The New Palace was the birthplace of the last

Am Neuen Palais
Apr–Oct Wed–Mon 10am–5:30pm, Nov/Dec Wed–Mon 10am–5pm, Jan–mar 10am–4:30pm
Tel. 969 42 00; www.spsg.de

▷ RE 1 Park Sanssouci, Bus X5, 605, 606, 695 Neues Palais

Majestic: Communs across from New Palace

Magnificent entrance to the Marble Hall: Marble Gallery

With Baroque pomp: Marble Hall

Demonstrating Prussia's new power: New Palace

(clockwise from top left)

two Prussian kings, both of whom became German emperors: Frederick III (1831–88) and William II (1859–1941). Frederick III died in the New Palace just three months after taking the throne. His son William II used the palace as his main residence from Easter to Christmas.

The **Temple of Friendship**, which Frederick the Great had erected in memory of his beloved sister Wilhelmine (1709–58), lies southeast of the New Palace. The statue in the open temple from 1768 depicts the Princess of Prussia – the later Margravine of Bayreuth – deep in thought.

Built as an architectural counterpoint to the other temple, the enclosed **Antique Temple**, northeast of the palace, was used by Frederick II to house his collection of art-works, coins and gems. It has served since 1828 as a mausoleum for members of the Hohenzollern family.

Impressive: view from colonnade of the Communs to New Palace

Captivating: Grotto Hall in the New Palace

In memory of Frederick's sister Wilhelmine: Temple of Friendship

Mausoleum and counterpart to the Friendship Temple: Antique Temple

(clockwise from above)

Nikolaikirche
St. Nicholas Church

The imposing cupola on the St. Nicholas Church can be seen from afar and dominates the silhouette of the city. The house of prayer, designed by Karl Friedrich Schinkel (1781–1841), is one of the most important works of classical architecture. The famous building master did not live to see its completion: for financial reasons, the church was dedicated without its planned dome in 1837, four years before his death. The 77-meter-high cupola with its tambour and surrounding columns was finally added in 1843–50 by Schinkel's pupils, Ludwig Persius and August Stüler, who employed a construction of cast iron, which was new at the time. The tambour's ring-shaped colonnade serves as a look-out platform.
The temple-like altar, baptismal font of black marble and the richly adorned pulpit from the time of Schinkel have been preserved inside the church hall. The rest of the church's interior, which was destroyed in World War II, was reconstructed in a more simple form in 1981. Parish rooms made of glass were built beneath the enlarged gallery.
The very first church in Potsdam was built at the site of the St. Nicholas Church in the 13th century. The original church was a Baroque structure built in 1721–24, but it burned down in 1795.

Am Alten Markt
Summer: open daily 10am–7pm, Winter: open daily 10am–5pm

▷ Tram 91, 92, 93, 96, 98, 99 Alter Markt/ Landtag

Work of Schinkel: Temple-like altar and pulpit

Masterpiece of Classicism: grand St. Nicholas Church

View into the church dome: portrayal of four Evangelists

(clockwise from top left)

Paretz
Paretz

Tracing the steps of the most popular monarch in Poland will lead you to Paretz in the Havelland region. The legendary Queen Luise (1776–1810) spent carefree summer weeks in the **Paretz Palace** with her husband King Frederick William III (1770–1840) and their children.
The palace was built by David Gilly in 1797, the year they ascended to the throne, and is a perfect example of early Prussian Classicism. Gilly also redesigned the town of Paretz in an aesthetically pleasing ensemble by 1805. The neo-Gothic **Village Church** and the **Gothic House** – once a blacksmith shop, now a restaurant – are well worth a look.
The treasures of the palace include the original wallpaper in the royal chambers. A highpoint of every visit is the exhibition "Coaches, Litters and Sleighs of the Prussian Royal Dynasty," presented in the **palace Carriage House**. Luise's wedding coach is a showpiece.
When Napoleon marched into Prussia in 1806, the idyllic visits to Paretz came to an end. After years in exile, Queen Luise returned to her beloved Paretz again in May 1810. The monarch, who had been venerated by the people, died two months later.

Parkring 1
14669 Ketzin / OT Paretz
Apr–Oct Tue–Sun 10a–5:30pm, Nov–Mar Sat/Sun 10am–4pm
033233/736 11; www.spsg.de

Carriage exhibition
Apr–Oct Tue–Sun 10am–6pm, Nov–Mar Sat/Sun 10am–4pm

▷ Bus 614, 650 Paretz

Neo-Gothic redesign: Paretz village church
Painted by hand: precious wall paper in garden hall of Paretz Palace
On display in the coach house: wedding coach of future Queen Luise
Puritanical posh: palace designed by Gilly
(clockwise from top left)

Pfingstberg

Pfingstberg

The Prussian monarchs could not make all their dreams for Potsdam come true. The **Belvedere** on the Pfingstberg, for example, remained a fragment. The structure, erected under King Frederick William IV (1795–1861), remains impressive nevertheless. Situated on a green hilltop, this monumental structure offers a breathtaking panoramic view over the Potsdam cultural landscape. This was the sole purpose of the building that was designed in the Italian Renaissance style with only two rooms. Three architects – Ludwig Persius, Friedrich August Stüler and Ludwig Ferdinand Hesse – were entrusted with the project in 1849–62. Both the casino and an immense cascade to the New Garden were never realized. A huge water basin was created in the courtyard of the Belvedere to serve as a reservoir for the planned water staircase.

A strong contrast is created by the **Temple of Pomona** beneath the Belvedere, which is small, modest, and delicate. The temple was built by Karl Friedrich Schinkel when he was just 19 and still unknown. He was commissioned to build the antique-style garden pavilion by the privy councilor Karl Ludwig von Oesfeld in 1800. The Temple of Pomona with its rooftop terrace was the first building of Schinkel's career.

Belvedere on the Pfingstberg
Pfingstberg
Apr–Oct open daily 10am–6pm, Nov/Mar Sat/Sun 10am–4pm
Information about tours: Tel. 20 05 79 30; www.pfingstberg.de

Pomona Temple
Easter–Oct Sat/Sun 12pm–5pm

▷ Tram 92, 96 Am Schragen, Bus 638 Am Pfingstberg

Stunning panoramic view: Belvedere on the Pfingstberg

Rich contrast: Belvedere and Pomona Temple

Oriental: hall ceiling of Moorish Cabinet in the Belvedere

One of only two rooms in the Belvedere: the Roman Cabinet

(clockwise from top left)

Ruinenberg und Historische Mühle

Ruinenberg and Historic Mill

As commander, Frederick II (1712–86) was tirelessly on the move, but he did not enjoy traveling during peacetime. He much preferred embellishing Potsdam with sceneries that gave him a feeling of far-away lands. The view from the court of honor in his → **Sanssouci** Palace, for example, looks over imitation antique Roman ruins, designed to perfection by the Italian theater painter Innocente Bellavite. The **Norman Tower** was added to the Ruinenberg ensemble in 1841–45. The only structure on the Ruinenberg that was actually meant to serve a function was the huge water basin, which was supposed to make the wells and fountains in Park Sanssouci spout water. But in the end the technical equipment failed. With the Historic Mill, Frederick II demonstrated his understanding of atmospheric imagery. The monarch regarded the simple secular structure next to his favorite palace as "ornamentation." That he was bothered by the clatter remains a legend. After Frederick's death, the mill was remodeled to resemble a Dutch windmill in 1791. The reconstructed mill serves today as a museum that shows how wind power was used around 1900 to grind and crush grain and turn it into flakes.

Historic Mill
Maulbeerallee 5
Apr–Oct open daily 10am–6pm, Nov, Jan–Mar Sat/Sun 10am–4pm
Tel. 550 68 51; www.historische-muehle-potsdam.de

▷ Bus X15, 695 Schloss Sanssouci, 692 Ruinenbergstraße

Inside the Norman Tower: exhibition on Ruinenberg

Central view of the Sanssouci Palace: Outlook from Norman Tower

Now a museum: Historic Mill at Sanssouci Palace

On a hilltop above the water basin: artfully-staged ruins

(clockwise from top left)

Russische Kolonie Alexandrowka
Russian Colony Alexandrowka

The royal houses of Hohenzollern and Romanov were joined in a friendly alliance through their joint recourse to take arms against Napoleon. After the death of Czar Alexander I (1777–1825), King Frederick William III (1770–1840) built a Russian village called Alexandrowka in Potsdam as a monument in his honor. Constructed in the north of the city center in 1827, it consisted of thirteen block houses, erected in the traditional Russian style with rustic timber and wood cut trimmings on the decorative gable facades. Peter Joseph Lenné, the garden director and designer of this unique ensemble, designed the ground plan in the shape of a hippodrome.

The Russian restaurant "Alexandrowka" lies at the main intersection. Another building houses the **Museum Alexandrowka**, providing information about the history and everyday life of the Russian colony. The landmarked colony, surrounded by fruit and vegetable gardens, has preserved its idyllic rural flair.

The **Alexander Newski Chapel** was built in 1829 for the first residents of the village – Russian singers in service of the Prussian king. The oldest Russian Orthodox church in western Europe was designed by Karl Friedrich Schinkel in collaboration with the Russian building master Wassilij Petrowitsch Stassow.

Museum Alexandrowka
Russische Kolonie 2
Daily 10am–6pm
Tel. 817 02 03; www.alexandrowka.de

Alexander Newski Chapel
Russische Kolonie 14
www.r-o-k.de

▷ Tram 92, 96 Puschkinallee, Bus 638 Reiterweg/Alleestraße

Offering typical Russian food: Restaurant in the Russian Colony

Like in old Russia: Stove with samovar in museum

On a hill: Alexander Newski Chapel

Showing life in the Russian Colony: Museum Alexandrowka

(clockwise from top left)

Sacrow
Sacrow

Sacrow is a peaceful oasis within Potsdam's cultural landscape and far away from the crowds of tourists. King Frederick William IV (1795–1861) purchased the estate in order to complete the idyllic royal arcadia around the Jungfernsee Lake. Today the **Sacrow Palace Park** appears wild and romantic. When garden architect Peter Joseph Lenné began designing the gardens in 1841, he paid special attention to the visual axes to Potsdam, Babelsberg and Glienicke.
The picturesque **Heilandskirche**, or Church of the Redeemer, was built inside the park on the bank of the Havel River in 1841–44. The architect Ludwig Persius designed the house of prayer in the style of an early Christian basilica with a circular colonnade. The separate campanile served in 1897 as an antenna base in the first successful attempts at broadcasting wireless radio in Germany. When Germany was divided, the church spent 28 years squeezed between the Berlin Wall and the Havel River in the no-man's land of the border. After the wall fell, the prayer services were held again for the first time on Christmas Eve 1989.
The poet Friedrich de la Motte Fouqué (1777–1843) spent his childhood in the Baroque **Sacrow Palace**. Cultural events are held here in the summer.

Sacrower Heilandskirche
Fährstrasse 1
Nov–Feb Sat/Sun 11am–3:30pm, May–Aug Tue–Thu 11am–4pm, Fri–Sun 11am–5pm, Sept, Oct, Mar, Apr Tue–Thu 11am–3:30pm, Fri–Sun 11am–4pm
www.heilandskirche-sacrow.de

Sacrow Palace
Hours vary according to exhibition. Tel. 969 42 00; www.spsg.de

▷ Bus 697 Schloss Sacrow

With a fantastic view of the Havel: Heilandskirche in Sacrow

Resembling a ship at anchor: church lying partly in riverbed

Kept simple: Inside the Heilandskirche

Surrounded by green: Sacrow Palace

(clockwise from top left)

Sanssouci, Schloss
Sanssouci Palace

King Frederick II (1712–86), the legendary 18th century monarch under whose reign Prussia became a major power, had no appreciation for the pomp and glamour of his fellow rulers. He chose not to build an opulent castle. Instead, at the start of his 46-year reign, he had a small summer palace erected on the vineyards west of the Potsdam city walls where he could relax and enjoy the warm months.

The artistically gifted monarch provided his own sketches to his architect and friend Georg Wenzeslaus von Knobelsdorff, who from 1745–47 built what would become the Hohenzollern dynasty's most famous palace. The jovial playful figures on the garden facade represent the god of wine's companions and underscore the motto of the superb Rococo structure: "Sans souci," without worries.

The Francophile Frederick summoned sophisticated intellectuals to his favorite palace so that they could engage in debates around his dining room table. For a time this legendary round table included the famous French philosopher Voltaire (1694–1778).

The interior design is imaginative and delicate, delighting with playful and cheerful Frederick-era Rococo. The decorative treasures were created by Johann August Nahl and the Hoppenhaupt brothers. Frederick the Great entertained

Maulbeerallee
Apr–Oct Tue–Sun 10am–5:30pm, Nov/Dec Tue–Sun 10am–5pm, Jan–Mar Tue–Sun 10am–4:30pm

Chinese House
May–Oct Tue–Sun 10am–5:30pm
Tel. 969 42 00; www.spsg.de

▷ Bus X15, 695 Schloss Sanssouci

Without worries: the name "Sans Souci" on the king's palace
Grand: Frederick held his round table in the Marble Hall
Legendary: the king played his flute in the concert room
Dynamic: Sanssouci Palace with vineyard terraces
(clockwise from top left)

his guests by playing flute in the opulently designed concert room.

The armchair in which "Old Fritz," as his subjects liked to call him, died on August 17, 1786, still stands in his study. His wish to be buried modestly, like "a philosopher," in a crypt at the palace, was finally fulfilled in 1991. Eleven of his dogs are buried with him in the simple grave.

A Baroque fruit and vegetable garden was laid around the palace and enlarged over time as new buildings were added. The current presentation of the Sanssouci Park as a landscape park was begun in 1818 by Peter Joseph Lenné. The end result was a total work of art which incorporates several buildings in addition to the Rococo palace, such as the → **New Palace**, → **New Orangery**, → **Picture Gallery** and → **Charlottenhof Palace**.

The **Chinese House** is another Rococo treasure. The exotic pavilion was also built on the basis of sketches by Frederick the Great in 1754–56. Gilded sandstone figures depicting Chinese people adorn the terraces and a golden mandarin sits on the roof.

Princely: room in the guest wing of palace

Sensual: Marble Venus on the Great Fountain

Equestrian sculpture: Frederick II in Sanssouci Park

Rococo with an Oriental flair: Chinese House of 1756

(clockwise from top left)

Schiffbauergasse, Kulturquartier

Schiffbauergasse Cultural Quarter

Potsdam shows its contemporary side in the Schiffbauergasse cultural quarter. Its landmark is the **Hans Otto Theater**, Potsdam's most important stage, which opened in 2006. The expressive curved facade is an eye catcher on the bank of the Tiefer See Lake. The new building created by the renowned Cologne architect Gottfried Böhm added a bold new performance venue to the stage that was founded in 1949. Near the theater, the Waveboard Boardinghouse, a hotel and apartment house, and the **Volkswagen Design Center** are both examples of new 21st century architecture.
The Schiffbauergasse Quarter is situated on the grounds of a former gas works on the periphery of the city. Coal gasification took place here from 1856–1990. A lively and colorful cultural life now thrives in the nearby landmarked halls of the former Hussar Barracks, with concert venues, the famous **Waschhaus**, cabaret, variety and dance theaters. The **Theaterschiff** is quite a special performance site. The **museum FLUXUS+** shows modern and contemporary art. The cultural district enjoys great popularity thanks to its diverse gastronomy and the lively area along the Havel riverbank.

Schiffbauergasse 4a–17
www.schiffbauergasse.de

▷ Tram 93, 94, 99 Schiffbauergasse

From gas works to cultural life: Schiffbauergasse

Exalting in color and form: Hans Otto Theater

Next door to the cultural center: Volkswagen Design Center

In the summer months: open-air stage in cultural quarter

(clockwise from above)

Stadtschloss (Landtag)
City Palace (Landtag)

When the City Palace was built, Potsdam became the royal seat of the Hohenzollern dynasty. The wish of the Great Elector (1620–88) to have a palace built in the small city on the Havel was realized in 1662–74. Three centuries later, in spring 1960, the leaders of East Germany tore down the war-damaged legacy of the monarchy.
In 2014, the City Palace again became a set piece in the old town of Potsdam. Brandenburg's future has been decided here since then too: the Brandenburg state parliament (Landtag) convenes behind the reconstructed facade – in modern rooms, of course. The city palace that we see today resembles the version that existed under Frederick II that was destroyed in World War II.
A few years after his coronation in 1744, the regent decided to make Potsdam his permanent residence. Over the course of eight years, the court architect Georg Wenzeslaus von Knobelsdorff built the city palace into a representative palace of the Prussian king's court. The blue roof was elaborately decorated with gold elements; vases and sculptures adorned the roof parapet. In honor of the coronation of Frederick I (1657–1713) as the first king of Prussia in 1701, the **Fortuna Portal** on the Old Market Square was integrated into the

Landtag Brandenburg
Am Alten Markt 1
Inner courtyard publicly accessible daily 8am–8pm,
Knobelsdorff Staircase, Cafeteria Mon–Fri 8am–6pm,
Rooftop terrace Mon–Fri 8am–10am, 1pm–6pm
Visitor Services: Tel. 966 12 60; www.landtag.brandenburg.de

▷ Tram 91, 92, 93, 96, 98, 99 Alter Markt/Landtag

Shaping the Potsdam old town again: reconstructed City Palace

Appealing to the ruler: petition tree on palace grounds

With original sandstone decoration: front of palace

With Prussian eagle: cartouche above portal

(clockwise from top left)

reconstruction as a symbol of the kingship. The splendid apartments of Frederick the Great reveled in elegant and playful Rococo forms. The royal chambers were located on the first floor and faced the Lange Brücke, the bridge across the Havel. Today, the plenary hall is situated at the site of the former banquet hall behind the palace ramp.
The **Pleasure Garden** began in front of the main entrance and is now nestled behind a hotel tower. Its design was based on its function as a recreational area and events location.
The **Neptune Fountain** contains fragments of the sculptural group "Neptune's Triumph" from the time of Frederick II.
Knobelsdorff also designed the **Ringerkolonnade**, a row of doubled columns, which originally connected the city palace with the royal stables (today's Film Museum). A segment has been erected here again.

Partially preserved: Neptune Fountain in the Pleasure Garden

Symbol of the Prussian kingdom: Fortuna Portal

Giving the portal its name: gilded goddess of fortune

Potsdam mix: City Palace with colonnade and East German high-rise hotel

(clockwise from top left)

Villenkolonie Babelsberg
Babelsberg Villa Colony

The → **Babelsberg Media Center** is not only famous for its role in making German film history; it is also the site of the affiliated celebrity district. UFA movie stars such as Lilian Harvey, Gustav Fröhlich and Marika Rökk lived in the elegant villa colony on Lake Griebnitzsee, not far from the film studios.
The actress Brigitte Horney put Erich Kästner up in her house at Johann-Strauss-Platz 11 in 1942. The author, who was disliked by the Nazi regime, secretly wrote screenplays under a pseudonym while he was here. Horney's residence had previously belonged to the Jewish industrialist Hans Gugenheim, who was forced to leave Germany in 1936.
At the end of the German empire, many industrialists, bankers and wealthy citizens from Berlin built luxurious villas on glorious lakeside properties. Many big name architects worked here, including Hermann Muthesius (Gugenheim house) and Ludwig Mies van der Rohe (Virchowstrasse 23).
During the Potsdam Conference in 1945, Josef Stalin resided in the Villa Herpich (Karl-Marx-Strasse 27) and Winston Churchill in Mies van der Rohe's Villa Urbig. Karl-Marx-Strasse 2 served as Harry S. Truman's "Little White House." The American president was in this villa when he issued the order to drop the bomb on the cities of Hiroshima and Nagasaki in August 1945. Today a **memorial stone** commemorates the more than 100,000 lives that were lost as a consequence of that decision.

Virchowstrasse, Karl-Marx-Strasse

Memorial for atomic bomb victims of 1945
Hiroshima-Nagasaki-Platz

▷ S 7 Griebnitzsee, Bus 694

Where Harry S. Truman resided in 1945: Villa Grote-Müller

Winston Churchill was a guest here: Villa Urbig

Josef Stalin was housed here: Villa Herpich

This is where 1930s film artists like Marlene Dietrich lived: Lilienthal-Burg

(clockwise from top left)

Weberviertel
Weavers Quarter

Prussia's rise was also the achievement of the crown's active immigration policy. The tranquil Weavers Quarter in Babelsberg was one of hundreds of new settlements created for immigrants under Frederick II. On behest of the king, the colony for weavers and spinners from Bohemia was founded in 1750. Persecuted in their home country for their Protestant beliefs, many families found a new home in the colony called "Nowawes" (Czech for "Neuendorf" or new village).

The streets on both sides of Karl-Liebknecht-Strasse in the landmarked Weavers Quarter are characterized by these modest, one-story residential homes, where two families would live. The **Friedrichskirche**, or Frederick's Church, on the expansive Weberplatz, was built in 1753 as a place of worship for Bohemian and German Protestants. It was designed by Jan Bouman the Elder.

The history of the village is presented in the museum **Nowaweser Weberstube**, in a former settler's house from 1752. The weavers lived under very humble conditions. The poor families lived and worked in a single room. Hardship in Nowawes led to frequent uprisings.

Nowaweser Weberstube
Karl-Liebknecht-Strasse 23
Tue–Thu 1pm–4pm
Tel. 50 03 74

▷ Tram 94, 99, Bus 694 Alt Nowawes, Rathaus Babelsberg

Spartan: original weavers house on Karl-Liebknecht-Strasse

Built for Protestants from Bohemia: Church of Peace on Weberplatz

Domicile for poor immigrants: two-family house in Weaver Quarter

Exhibition on life in the colony: Nowaweser Weberstube

(clockwise from top left)

24

Wissenschaftspark Albert-Einstein
Albert Einstein Science Park

The **Einstein Tower**, named after the genius Albert Einstein (1879–1955), looks like a futuristic monument. The unusual structure was erected in 1920–22 to prove Einstein's theory of relativity. The sun observation station designed by the architect Erich Mendelsohn is a world famous masterpiece of expressionist architecture and the highpoint of the Albert Einstein Science Park.
On the wooded hill called **Telegrafenberg**, illustrious institutes conduct research on the universe, the earth, oceans and on local and worldwide climate change. The **Astrophysical Observatory** from the time of the emperor is very impressive. The domed structure from 1899 contains the world's fourth largest refracting telescope. Next door, on the highest point of the Telegrafenberg, the architect Paul Emanuel Spieker built another complex to investigate the mysteries of outer space. Telegrafenberg, the name of the hill south of the city center, goes back to a telegraph station used by the Russian military. A replica of **Station No. 4** – one of 62 stations established to transmit information between Berlin and Koblenz in 1842–59 – recalls how communication was once carried out using visual signals.

Telegrafenberg / Albert-Einstein-Strasse
Publicly accessible grounds

Einstein Tower
Viewings in winter only
To book tours: www.urania-potsdam.de

▷ Bus 691 Telegrafenberg

Traditional geodesic research center: Helmert building on Telegrafenberg

Centerpieces of the science park: Astrophysical Observatory and Einstein Tower (below)

Shaped like a clover leaf: Helmholtz Center of Geological Research

Observation station for the sun: Einstein Tower

(clockwise from top left)

Service

POTSDAM AREA CODE

When calling from outside Potsdam, first dial the area code 0331.

POTSDAM INFO

The state capital's official website www.potsdam.de provides information on museums, events and special programs.
www.info-potsdam.de is a useful address for finding hotels and also provides information on culture, restaurants, sports etc.
Another informative address is www.potsdam-abc.de, with up-to-date news on current topics and events.
The official internet site for tourists is www.potsdam-tourismus.de. It contains information on walking and bus tours, sightseeing attractions and palaces. Rooms in hotels and bed-and-breakfasts can be booked directly online, by phone (27 55 88 99) or email to info@potsdamtourismus.de.
There are three tourist information offices in the city center: On the Old Market Square (Humboldtstrasse 1–2, Mon–Sat 9:30am–7pm, Sun 10am–4pm), in the main train station (Babelsberger Strasse 16, passageway to the tracks, Mon–Sat 9:30am–6pm) and on Luisenplatz 3 (corner of Allee nach Sanssouci, Mon–Sat 9:30am–6pm, Apr–Oct and Sun 10am–4pm).

INFO ON PALACES AND GARDENS

Current information about the palaces and buildings of the Prussian crown (visiting times, addresses, renovations, exhibitions etc.) is found on the Prussian Palaces and Gardens Foundation website (www.spsg.de). The phone number for visitor information is 969 42 00.
The SPSG has two visitor centers in Park Sanssouci: The visitors center at the Historic Mill (An der Orangerie 1, 14469, Brandenburger Vorstadt) is open daily Mar–Oct 8:30am–5pm, Nov–Feb 9am–4pm; the visitors center at the New Palace (Am Neuen Palais 3, 14469, Brandenburger Vorstadt) is open Apr–Oct Wed–Mon 9am–6pm, Nov–Mar Wed–Mon 10am–5pm.
With the Ticket sanssouci+ (ca. 19 euros) one can visit all the Potsdam palaces (except Sacrow Palace and Stern Hunting Lodge) on any single day. There is also the Ticket sanssouci+ Familie for families. It is advisable to book entrance tickets in advance at www.spsg.de.

CHOOSING A HOTEL

The website www.hotels-potsdam.de can be used to search for suitable accommodations and make reservations (tel. 23 70 00 92, Mon–Fri 12pm–7pm).
Two other websites are also helpful: www.potsdam-tourismus.de and www.info-potsdam.de.
Offers for a double room begin at 60–70 euros.

TICKETS

Tickets for cultural events can be booked online at www.ticketeria.de.
The centrally located concert and theater box offices are: Konzert- & Theaterkasse in the train station passageway, Babelsberger Strasse 16, 14473, Südliche Innenstadt, Mon–Sat 9:30am–8pm, tel. 09001/14 00 11, www.bahnhofspassagen-potsdam.de
PNN-Shop in the Wilhelmgalerie, Platz der Einheit, 14467, Nördliche Innenstadt, tel. 237 62 22, Mon–Fri 10am–6pm, www.pnn.de
MAZ Media Store, Friedrich-Ebert-Strasse 85/86, 14467, Nördliche Innenstadt, tel. 284 01 40, Mon–Fri 9am–7pm, Sat 9am–4pm, www.my-mediastore.de/potsdam.

FIRST AID, LOST AND FOUND

Police/emergency assistance: tel. 110; Fire dept./emergency rescue: tel. 112; medical assistance: tel. 11 61 17; city lost and found (Friedrich-Ebert-Strasse 79–81, 14469, Nauener Vorstadt): Mon 10am–6pm, Tue–Thu 8am–6pm, Fri 8am–2pm, tel. 289 15 87, www.potsdam.de; ViP transit company lost and found (Fritz-Zubeil-Strasse 96, 14482, Babelsberg Süd): Mon–Wed 9:30am–8pm, Thu 9:30am–4pm, Fri 9:30am–5pm, tel. 661 45 55, www.vip-potsdam.de.

CITY TOURS

Bus Tours

Bus tours begin either at Luisenplatz or in front of the main train station on Babelsberger Strasse.
The Potsdam City Tour, which begins at Luisenplatz, allows passengers to enter and exit the bus at different stations along the tour, for example at the Sanssouci Palace (tel. 97 43 76, www.potsdam-city-tour.de). The same company offers city and palace circle tours without interruptions that depart at the main train station on Babelsberger Strasse (www.schloesserrundfahrten.de). The Potsdam Kaiser Tour also starts at the main train station on Babelsberger Strasse (tel. 71 09 90, www.kaiser-tour.de).

Bike Tours

Pedales offers guided sightseeing bike tours on weekends. Tours begin at the Radstation at the main train station (Babelsberger Strasse, tel. 748 00 57, www.pedales.de).

Havel Boat Tour

The boat company "Weisse Flotte Potsdam" offers popular boat tours on the lakes of the Havel River. The main boarding dock is across from the City Palace (Lange Brücke 6, 14467, Südliche Innenstadt, tel. 275 92 10, www.schifffahrt-in-potsdam.de). It offers a large selection of trips including circle tours to the palaces (at night too) as well as day trips around Potsdam or to Berlin. The peak season is April to October. Ships don't operate in January and February. Schedule information is also provided by phone (275 92 33).

Walking Tours

Walking tours along the former city gates are offered by Kades TorTour, meeting point at Brandenburg Gate (tel. 29 35 33, www.restaurant-pfingstberg.de) and by the Potsdamer Nachtwächter (tel. 0160/ 95 67 66 46, www.potsdamer-nachtwaechter.de).

Costumed guides portraying historic figures or footmen of the Prussian royal household discuss life in the Prussian court. These performed tours take place on Sundays in Park Sanssouci and Park Babelsberg and are offered by the Prussian Palaces and Gardens Foundation: www.spsg.de/kalender or tel. 969 42 22.

PUBLIC TRANSPORTATION

S-Bahn, Tram and Bus

S-Bahn, trams, buses and ferries run in the Potsdam metropolitan area. The same ticket can be used for any means of transport run by the Potsdam Transport Company (ViP) and the Berlin-Brandenburg Transport System (VBB). The VBB ticket is also valid on all local trains connecting Potsdam with Berlin.
Trams and buses run on weekdays from 5am to 11pm. A few lines run until 1am. Special night buses run daily on Lines N13, N14, N16 und N17. Two other lines (N15, N43) only run on Friday and Saturday nights. The Potsdam transport system is divided into three price groups: Zone A, B (city area) and C (outskirts). Tickets can be purchased from ticket machines in trams and buses (60 minutes in a single direction), 4-trip tickets or a day ticket. ViP customer centers are found at the main train station (southern front plaza) and in the Wilhelmgalerie (Platz der Einheit). They are open Mon–Fri 7am–7pm and Sat 9am–2:30pm. Information on Potsdam public transportation and ferry schedules are available online at www.vip-potsdam.de and by phone: ViP-info-tel. 661 42 75; emergency calls 661 43 33.
Visit Berlin offers a Potsdam version of the Berlin WelcomeCard, which covers all zones of Potsdam and Berlin (price zones ABC). WelcomeCard ticketholders can use the public transportation and also receive discounts on 29 cultural events and tourist attractions in Potsdam (200 offers if Berlin is included). The tickets are valid from 48 hours (ca. 22 euros) to

6 days (ca. 46 euros). More information online at www.berlin-welcomecard.de. The WelcomeCard is available at tourist information offices and sales offices of the Potsdam transport system.

Water Taxis
Water taxis run on the Potsdam waterways on set routes and schedules. There are 13 stations on the Havel River and Havel lakes. Tickets are sold on board and cost 3.50 euros for one trip; a day ticket costs 16 euros. The water taxi season begins in the spring and ends in October.
Boats run daily except from mid-October and mid-April when they only run on the weekends.
The main dock for water taxis is at Lange Brücke 6, 14467, Südliche Innenstadt, tel. 275 92 10, www.potsdamer-wassertaxi.de.

Taxis
Taxi companies in Potsdam are City Funk Potsdam (tel. 81 04 04, www.taxi-potsdam.com), Taxi-Zentrale Potsdam (tel. 29 29 29, www.taxi-potsdam.de) and Rainer Gross (tel. 20 15 90, www.potsdam-taxi.de).

Velotaxis
Rikscha Potsdam offers an environmentally friendly taxi alternative (tel. 0178/795 62 78, rikscha-potsdam.de.tl). An hour trip costs 30 euros, 25 euros for each addition hour.

Bike Rentals
In addition to the bike rental service provided by Deutsche Bahn, there is also Rad Station, another large bike rental company (main train station, Babelsberger Strasse exit, Mon–Fri 7am–8pm, Sat 9:30am–7pm, Sun 9:30am–7pm on the S-Bahn platform, tel. 748 00 57, www.pedales.de, mail@pedales.de).
n the Griebnitzsee Station you can rent bikes as well as kayaks and go paddling on Griebnitzsee Lake (Apr–Oct Mon–Fri 9am–6:30pm, Sat/Sun 9am–7pm, Nov–Mar Mo–Fri 9am–6pm).

CULTURE

Museum
The MUSEUM combi-ticket is good for four museums (Film Museum, House of Brandenburg-Prussian History, Natural History Museum and Potsdam Museum).
It costs ca. 12 euros and can be purchased in the museums or at the tourist information office.
The *Film Museum Potsdam* presents the beginnings of filmmaking and its evolution (Breite Strasse 1A, 14467, Nördliche Innenstadt, Tue–Sun 10am–6pm, tel. 271 81 12, www.filmmuseum-potsdam.de).
The eventful history of the Prussian Garrison Church is presented in the *Cross of Nails Chapel* (Breite Strasse 7, 14467, Nördliche Innenstadt, Tue–Sun 11am–5pm, tel. 201 18 30, www.garnisonkirche-potsdam.de).
The course of history in the Mark Brandenburg region is traced in the *House of Brandenburg-Prussian History* (Am Neuen Markt 9, 14467, Nördliche Innenstadt, Tue–Thu 10am–5pm, Fri–Sun 10am–6pm, tel. 620 85 50, www.hbpg.de).
See how a miller worked in olden times in the *Historic Mill* (Maulbeerallee 5, 14469, Brandenburger Vorstadt, Apr–Oct open daily 10am–6pm, Nov, Jan–Mar Sat/Sun 10am–4pm, tel. 550 68 51, www.historische-muehle-potsdam.de).
Earthenware and ceramics, once important objects of daily life, are on display in the Baroque house *"Im Güldenen Arm"* (Hermann-Elflein-Strasse 3, 14467, Nördliche Innenstadt, Wed–Sun 12pm–6pm, tel. 0176/10 00 65 04, www.imgueldenenarm.de).
18th century everyday life in the Dutch Quarter is the focus of the *Jan Bouman House* (Mittelstrasse 8, 14467, Nördliche Innenstadt, Mon–Fri 1pm–6pm, Sat/Sun 11am–6pm, tel. 280 37 73, www.jan-bouman-haus.de).
Earlier times in the Russian Village is shown in *Museum Alexandrowka* (Russische Kolonie 2, 14469, Nauener Vorstadt, open daily 10am–6pm, tel. 817 02 03, www.alexandrowka.de).
The *Museum of Natural History* delves into native wildlife (Breite Strasse 13, 14467, Nördliche Innenstadt, Tue–Sun 9am–5pm, tel. 289 67 07, www.naturkundemuseum-potsdam.de).
The weavers' austere work world is presented in the *Nowaweser Weberstube* (Karl-Liebknecht-Strasse 23, 14482, Babelsberg Nord, Tue–Thu 1pm–4pm, tel. 50 03 74).
The *Potsdam Museum* presents the moving history of the royal city and seat of power (Am Alten Markt 9, 14467, Nördliche Innenstadt, Tue–Fri 10am–5pm, Thu 10am–7pm, Sat/Sun 10am–6pm, tel. 289 68 68, www.potsdam-museum.de).

The *Potsdamer Zinnfigurenmuseum* shows its collection of miniature tin figures (Krongut Bornstedt, Ribbeckstrasse 6–7, 14469, Bornstedt, open daily 10am–6pm, tel. 60 05 19 60, www.krongut-bornstedt.de).

Palaces and Gardens

Information on all the Potsdam palaces is provided by phone 969 42 00 or online www.spsg.de.

Sanssouci Palace, the favorite palace of Frederick the Great, is located in *Park Sanssouci* (Maulbeerallee, 14469, Brandenburger Vorstadt, Apr–Oct Tue–Sun 10am–5:30pm, Nov/Dec Tue–Sun 10am–5pm, Jan–Mar Tue–Mon 10am–4:30pm, tickets with set entry times). The king's neighboring guesthouse is called *Neue Kammern* (Apr–Oct Tue–Sun 10am–5:30pm). The palace kitchen can also be viewed (Apr–Oct Tue–Sun 10am–6pm).

Frederick II's largest palace is the *New Palace* (Am Neuen Palais, 14469, Brandenburg outskirts, Apr–Oct Wed–Mon 10am–5:30pm, Nov/Dec Wed–Mon 10am–5pm, Jan–Mar Wed–Mon 10am–4:30pm, tickets with set entry times).

King Frederick William IV built the *Charlottenhof Palace* in Sanssouci (Geschwister-Scholl-Strasse 34a, 14471, Brandenburger Vorstadt, May–Oct Tue–Sun 10am–5:30pm), not far from the Italian-looking Roman Baths (May–Oct Tue–Sun 10am–5:30pm).

The *New Orangery* was also erected under Frederick William IV (An der Orangerie 3–5, 14469, Brandenburger Vorstadt, Apr Sat/Sun 10am–6pm, May–Oct Tue-Sun 10am–6pm).

The classical *Marble Palace* is situated in the New Garden, which was created under Frederick William II (Im Neuen Garten 10, 14469, Nauener Vorstadt, May–Oct Tue–Sun 10am–6pm, Nov–Mar Sat/Sun 10am–4pm, in Apr Sat/Sun 10am–6pm). *Cecilienhof Palace* was built just shortly before the end of the monarchy (In Neuen Garten 11, 14469, Nauener Vorstadt, Apr–Oct Tue–Sun 10am–5:30pm, Nov/Dec Tue–Sun 10am–5pm, Jan–Mar Tue–Sun 10am–4:30pm).

Babelsberg Palace, the summer residence of Emperor William I, lies in *Park Babelsberg* (Park Babelsberg 10, 14482, Babelsberg Nord, irregular hours due to ongoing renovations, check online at www.spsg.de). The *Flatow Tower* (Park Babelsberg 12, 14482, Babelsberg Nord, May–Oct Sat/Sun 10am–5pm) served as his private realm.

Two palaces which are listed as World Cultural Heritage sites are situated within the Berlin city limits: The *Glienicke Palace* in Glienicke Park (Königstrasse 36, 14109 Berlin, Apr–Oct Tue–Sun 10am–5:30pm, Nov/Dec Sat/Sun 10am–5pm, Mar Sat/Sun 10am–4pm) and the *Peacock Island Palace* on Peacock Island, Frederick Williams II's retreat, offering a view of the New Garden (Nikolskoer Weg, 14109 Berlin, Apr–Oct Tue–Sun 10am–5:30pm).

The little *Stern Hunting Lodge* was built by soldier king Frederick William I. (Jagdhausstrasse 1A, 14480, Am Stern, open during events. Call for information and appointments: tel. 58 29 11 37, www.jagdschloss-stern.de).

Caputh Palace is the oldest palace in Potsdam, built during the time of Frederick William of Brandenburg (Strasse der Einheit 2, 14548 Caputh, tel. 033209/703 45, Apr–Oct Tue–Sun 10am–5:30pm, Nov–Mar Sat/Sun 10am–4pm).

Paretz Palace was the favorite site of Queen Luise of Prussia and her husband Frederick William III (Parkring 1, 14669 Ketzin / OT Paretz, 033233/736 11, Apr–Oct Tue–Sun 10am–5:30pm, Nov–Mar Sat/Sun 10am–4pm).

Art

Information about current exhibitions available online at www.kunst-potsdam.de.

Potsdam's two outstanding painting museums are the *Picture Gallery* (Im Park Sanssouci 4, 14469, Brandenburger Vorstadt, May–Oct Tue–Sun 10am–5:30pm, tel. 969 42 00, www.spsg.de) and *Museum Barberini* (Humboldtstrasse 5–6, 14467, Nördliche Innenstadt, Wed–Mon 10am–7pm, open every first Thursday in the month from 10am–9pm, tel. 236 01 44 99, www.museum-barberini.com).

Modern and contemporary art is presented in *museum FLUXUS+* (Schiffbauergasse 4f, 14467, Berliner Vorstadt, Wed–Sun 1pm–6pm, tel. 60 10 89 30, www.fluxus-plus.de).

Changing contemporary art exhibitions are shown in the Exhibition *Pavilion on Friendship Island* (Lange Brücke, 14467, Südliche Innenstadt, Wed–Sun 1pm-

5pm, tel. 279 75 39 80, www.bkv-potsdam.de); in *Kunstraum Potsdam* (Schiffbauergasse 4d, 14467, Berliner Vorstadt, Wed–Sun 1pm–6pm, tel. 73 09 89 93, www.kunstraumpotsdam.de); in *Kunstverein Kunst-Haus* (Ulanenweg 9, 14469, Jägervorstadt, Tue 11am–3pm, Wed–Fri 11am–6pm, Sat/Sun 12pm–5pm, tel. 200 80 86, www.kunstverein-kunsthaus-potsdam.de); and in the *Villa Schöningen* (Berliner Strasse 86, 14467, Berliner Vorstadt, Wed–Sun 12pm–6pm, Thu 12pm–8pm, tel. 200 17 41, www.villa-schoeningen.de).
A popular location for experimental art is the *Rechenzentrum Kunst- und Kreativhaus* (Dortustrasse 46, 14467, Nördliche Innenstadt, hours vary according to exhibition, tel. 74 79 70, www.rz-potsdam.de).

Theater, Dance and Concerts
The largest non-musical theater in Potsdam is the *Hans Otto Theater* (Schiffbauergasse 11, 14467, Berliner Vorstadt, box office Mon–Fri 10am–6pm, Sat 10am–2pm, tel. 981 18, www.hansottotheater.de).
The important stages for cabaret, variety and youth theater are *Theaterschiff* (Schiffbauergasse 9b, 14467, Berliner Vorstadt, tickets: tel. 97 23 02, www.theaterschiff-potsdam.de) and *T-Werk* (Schiffbauergasse 4e, 14467, Berliner Vorstadt, tel. 71 91 39, www.t-werk.de).
Dance theater is presented by *fabrik Potsdam* (Schiffbauergasse 10, 14467, Berliner Vorstadt, tel. 280 03 14, www.fabrikpotsdam.de).
The most important concert halls are the *Nikolaisaal* (Wilhelm-Staab-Strasse 10–11, 14467, Nördliche Innenstadt, tickets: Mon–Fri 11am–6pm, Sat 11am–2pm, tel. 288 88 28, www.nikolaisaal.de) and the *Waschhaus* (Schiffbauergasse 6, 14467, Berliner Vorstadt, tel. 27 15 60, www.waschhaus.de).

Memorials
Resistance against Hitler by Wehrmacht officers is documented in the exhibition *Potsdam and the 20th of July 1944* (in the Ministry of Infrastructure and Agriculture, Henning-von-Tresckow-Strasse 2–8, 14467, Nördliche Innenstadt, Mon–Fri 9am–4pm, tel. 289 68 00, www.potsdam.de).
The conference room in the *Cecilienhof Palace* is an historic site of the 1945 Potsdam Conference (Im Neuen Garten 11, 14469, Nauener Vorstadt, Apr–Oct Tue–Sun 10am–5:30pm, Nov/Dec Tue–Sun 10am–5pm, Jan–Mar Tue–Sun 10–4:30, tel. 969 42 00, www.spsg.de).
The activities and consequences of the secret service in the Cold War are the focus of the *Leistikowstrasse Memorial and Meeting Place* (Leistikowstrasse 1, 14469, Nauener Vorstadt, Apr–Oct Tue–Sun 2pm–6pm, Nov–Mar Tue–Sun 1pm–5pm, tel. 201 15 40, www.gedenkstaette-leistikowstrasse.de); the *History Trail of the Soviet Secret Service "Military Town No. 7"* (Grosse Weinmeisterstrasse, Am Neuen Garten, 14469, Nauener Vorstadt); and the *Villa Schöningen* on the famous Glienicke Bridge (Exhibition "Spies. Wall. Children's Home," Berliner Strasse 86, 14467, Berliner Vorstadt, Wed–Sun 12pm–6pm, open Thursday until 8pm, tel. 200 17 41, www.villa-schoeningen.de).
The persecution and crimes committed during the Nazi dictatorship, the Soviet occupation and the SED dictatorship are documented in the *Lindenstrasse Memorial Foundation* in the former prison of the East German Stasi (Lindenstrasse 54, 14467, Nördliche Innenstadt, Tue–Sun 10am–6pm, tel. 289 61 12, www.gedenkstaette-lindenstrasse.de).

Nature and Film
The *Botanical Gardens* (Maulbeerallee 2, 14469, Bornstedt, Apr–Sept open daily 9:30am–5pm, Oct–Mar open daily 9:30am–4pm, outdoor areas open 8am to dusk, tel. 977 19 36, www.botanischer-garten-potsdam.de) lie within Park Sanssouci. The *Karl Foerster Garden*, the flowering paradise of the well-known plant breeder Karl Foerster, is situated in the Bornim city district (Am Raubfang 6, 14469, Bornim, open daily 9am to dusk, www.foerster-stauden.de).
To get a closer look at the stars, visit the *Urania Planetarium* (Gutenbergstrasse 71–72, 14467, Nördliche Innenstadt, tel.: 270 27 21, program and event schedule online at www.urania-planetarium.de).
Take a peek behind the scenes of the film industry and marvel at special effects and stunts in *Filmpark Babelsberg* (entrance: Grossbeerenstrasse 200, 14482, Babelsberg Süd, Apr–Sept 10am–6pm, Oct 10am–5pm, tel. 721 23 45 (tickets), 721 27 50 (info hotline), www.filmpark-babelsberg.de).

SALVE

Index of sites

Index of artists and architects

VBB **Potsdam**

Tageslinienetz *Daytime Network* ABC Tarifbereich Potsdam ABC *tariff area of Potsdam*

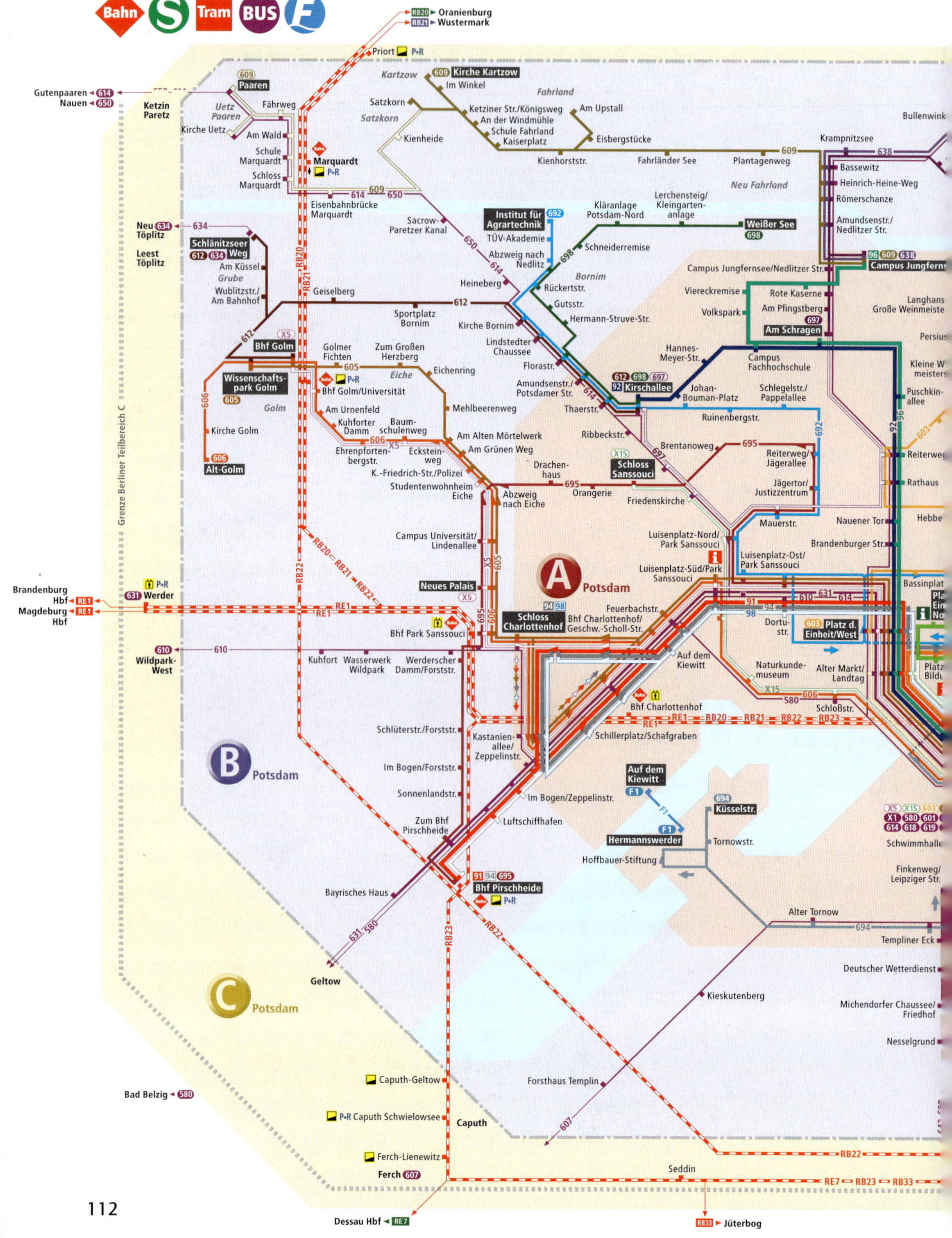